SALE, Richard
Owain Glyndwr's Way

Owain Glyndwr's Way

By the same author for Constable

A Cambrian Way
A guide to the Cleveland Way
A guide to the Cotswold Way
Holding the heights
Best walks in North Wales
Best walks in Southern Wales
Best walks in the South-West

Owain Glyndwr's Way

Richard Sale

Constable · London

First published in Great Britain 1992
by Constable and Company Limited
3 The Lanchesters, 162 Fulham Palace Road
London W6 9ER
Copyright © 1992 Richard Sale
The right of Richard Sale to be identified
as the author of this work has been
asserted by him in accordance with the
Copyright, Designs and Patents Act 1988
ISBN 0 09 471310 3
Set in Linotron 9pt Palatino by
CentraCet, Cambridge
Printed in Great Britain by
Butler and Tanner Limited, Frome

A CIP catalogue record for this book
is available from the British Library

To the memory of my father, who loved mid-Wales.

Contents

Illustrations

Maps

Acknowledgements

The author gratefully acknowledges the help of the National University of Wales and the library service of Powys County Council in the research underlying this book. He is also grateful for the assistance of officers of Powys County Council for their help over matters to do with the route itself.

Finally he is especially grateful to Tony Oliver for his assistance on and off the route, and particularly for the use of some of his photographs.

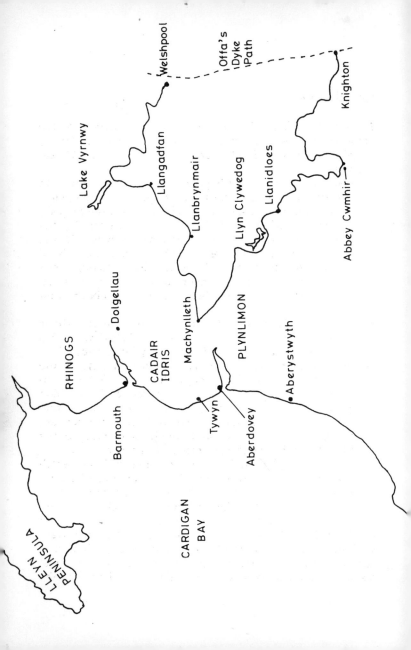

Introduction

The Marble Hall of Cardiff's Town Hall is reserved for the heroes of the Welsh nation. Here there are statues of St David, Dafydd ap Gwilym, Esgob Morgan, Hywel Da – and Owain Glyndwr.

Owain Glyndwr lived during the latter half of the fourteenth and the early years of the fifteenth century. In those first years of the fifteenth century he led a rebellion against the English, during which the land of Wales was devastated by the 'scorched earth' policy of Owain and his followers. In the wake of the unsuccessful revolt, which left thousands of young men, Welsh and English, dead,. Wales was oppressed by punitive laws enacted to ensure that never again would the Welsh rise to trouble their English neighbours and overlords.

Why then is Owain Glyndwr a hero of the nation? Why is he revered as a symbol of freedom for Wales, when his rebellion led to what was effectively slavery for its people?

This book cannot answer these questions directly, for the answer lies buried in the psyche of the Welsh. What it can and does do, however, is to set out the history of the rebellion and place it in the context of the history of Wales both before and after Glyndwr. The aims and conduct of the rebellion are set down, so that the reader can form his own opinion of the judgement that the Welsh have made on this man.

In order to explore fully Glyndwr's aims and the Welsh hopes at the time of the rebellion, it is necessary to understand something of Wales. To do that, there is no better way than to follow the route that Powys County Council have way-marked through the county and named after the rebel Welsh prince. This walk (soon to be designated a National Trail) starts at Knighton on Offa's Dyke, still on the English border, near the battlefield of Pilleth where the Welsh had their most decisive victory. It visits Abbey Cwmhir where Llywelyn the

Waymarker

Last lies buried, and the uplands of Plynlimon where Glyndwr raised his standard and also won his first victory over the English. The route then runs on to Machynlleth where Owain held the first parliament of his free Wales, before heading towards the Welsh upland again, this time to the Berwyns and Lake Vyrnwy. Beyond is Mathrafal, home of the Welsh Princes of Powys from whom Owain was descended, then Welshpool with its Red Castle, symbolic of Norman England. Map references within the text refer to Ordnance Survey maps (see Maps and Waymarking p. 16).

In addition to following the history of Owain's rebellion, Glyndwr's Way passes through some of the finest scenery in mid-Wales. While this area does not have the grandeur of the mountains in Snowdonia nor the stark beauty of the scarp slopes in the Brecon Beacons National Park, it does boast the wooded vales of Radnor, the Clywedog valley, the unspoilt areas of old Montgomeryshire and, along the River Dyfi, perhaps the loveliest river valley in Wales.

When Daniel Defoe visited Wales he paused at Bwlch-y-groes, the pass between Bala and the valley of the Dyfi, a little way west of Lake Vyrnwy. He surveyed the 'horrid and frightful' hills and decided that 'the Devil lives in the middle of Wales'. Later, Dr Johnson came and decided that 'Wales is so little different from England that it offers nothing to the speculation of the traveller'.

Had Defoe known of the *canwyll y corph*, the corpse candles whose light can be seen flickering across the hillsides as they make their way to the houses of those who will die, or of the *Aderyn y Corph*, the corpse bird that shrieks at night for the same ghastly purpose, or seen the hill farmers killing black sheep for fear they were the devil in disguise, his belief would have been strengthened.

Had Johnson known that at Llanwnog it is held that if a magpie flies from right to left it will bring bad luck, whereas if it flies from left to right it will bring good luck, or that if a heron is seen flying upriver it will rain because the bird flies upstream to bring the rain down, he would still perhaps have been unimpressed.

Defoe and Johnson also spoke of the scenery but were wrong about that too.

Those who travel Glyndwr's Way will explore a country rich in history, myth and legend, and see some of the finest scenery in Britain at first hand. Perhaps too they will understand a little more of this most enigmatic of Welsh leaders.

THE WELSH LANGUAGE

The Celtic language that crossed to Britain from continental Europe split into two variants; the Goidelic language of Ireland, Scotland and the Isle of Man, and the Brythonic language of Wales and Cornwall. The two variants are now differentiated as 'Q Celtic' – Goidelic Celtic or Gaelic – and 'P Celtic' – Welsh, Cornish, and Breton, the similar language of Britany. The reason for the definition is in the pronounciation of 'qu'. Q Celtic pronounces this as 'c', while P Celtic pronounces it as 'p'. An easy illustration of the difference can be seen in the word for 'mountain'. Welsh has *pen*, while Gaelic has *ceann*.

To the English eye, the Welsh language is an unreadable mass of vowel-less words, consonants back-to-back. This impression is based on the misconception that the alphabets of the two languages are the same. In fact Welsh has extra consonants, 'dd', 'll' and 'ff' being letters – not as strange as it seems, for remember that English has 'w', i.e. uu – and can utilise 'w' and 'y' as vowels. While 'dd' (pronounced 'th') and 'll' (pronounced 'thl') have their own sounds, 'ff' is pro-

nounced 'f', for the Welsh 'f' sounds like a 'v'. Thus Tryfan is
pronounced 'Tryvaen' and *cwm* (a corrie or mountain hollow)
is pronounced 'coom'. A second, radical departure from
English is initial mutation which is the alteration of the initial
consonants of words when the final sound of the preceding
word is of particular form. The reason for this appears to be
aesthetic. However, the (apparently random) interchangeabil-
ity of, say, *fawr* and *mawr* (large) or *fach* and *bach* (small), not
to mention other worse forms, e.g. *cam – gam – ngham – cham*,
makes the casual observer wince.

Throughout the book the common form of place-names has
been used, even when this has meant using an English version
rather than the orthodox Welsh.

An attempt at a comprehensive glossary of useful Welsh
words is obviously doomed to failure, but the following is, I
hope, a useful short list to allow walkers a better understand-
ing of the ground they cover.

Aber, confluence, but usually a river mouth
Afon, river
Allt (*Gallt*), hill, especially if wooded
Bach (*Fach, Bychan*), small
Bedd, grave
Betws, chapel
Blaen, head of valley
Bont, bridge
Braich, arm
Bwlch, pass
Cadair, chair
Caer, fort
Capel, chapel
Carn (*Carnedd*), a pile of stones
Carreg, stone
Castell, castle
Cau, deep hollow

Cefn, ridge
Clogwyn, cliff
Coch (Goch), red
Coed, wood
Craig, crag
Crib, comb, narrow ridge
Cwm, mountain hollow, a valley with a backslope, as used in the famous Western Cwm below Everest
Dinas, town or hill-fort
Du (Ddu), black
Dwr, water
Dyffryn, valley
Eglwys, church
Eira, snow
Esgair, long ridge
Ffordd, road, pathway
Ffynnon, well, spring
Glas (Las), blue-green
Gribin, jagged ridge
Gwynt, wind
Hafod, summer dwelling, hillside house for summer use
Hen, old
Hendre, winter dwelling, valley house for winter use
Hir, long
Isaf, lowest
LLech, flat stone
Llethr, slope
Llithrig, slippery
Llyn, lake
Maen, stone (*maen hir*, long stone or standing stone, i.e. menhir)
Mawr (Fawr), big
Moel (Foel), bare, rounded hill
Mynydd (Fynydd), mountain
Nant, stream, brook
Newydd, new
Ogof, cave

Pant, small hollow
Pen, peak
Pistyll, waterfall, usually a water spout
Pont (*Bont*), bridge
Porth, gate
Pwll, pool
Rhaeadr, waterfall
Rhyd, ford
Saeth, arrow
Sarn, causeway
Sych, dry
Tref, town
Twll, hole
Ty, house
Uchaf, highest
Waun, moor
Wen or *Gwyn*, white
Y (*Yr*), the, of the
Ynys, island
Ysgol, ladder

MAPS AND WAYMARKING

Although Owain Glyndwr eventually took the four lions of
Gwynedd as his coat of arms, he fought initially under the
arms of the princes of Powys from whom he was descended.
Ffordd Glyndwr – the route through the county of Powys that
bears Owain's name – has been created by linking together
existing rights of way, sometimes by using minor roads. At
one or two points, most noticeably near Machynlleth, major
roads are used. The Countryside Council for Wales (the Welsh
arm of the Countryside Commission), when suggesting long-
distance footpaths (now called National Trails) for official
designation by Act of Parliament, has the power to create new
rights of way. Powys County Council had no such authority
when creating Glyndwr's Way and has endeavoured to

explore the history and scenery of the county to the full using the present path network. They are also continually trying to improve the Way and minor variations to the route described in this book may be encountered.

Recently, the CCW has decided to make Glyndwr's Way a National Trail. Their decision is to be welcomed: no long-distance footpath lies wholly within Wales (Offa's Dyke Path is shared with England) and the route travels through some outstanding scenery. Present CCW policy is to start consultations with interested parties – walking groups, farmers, etc. – in the Spring of 1992, with a view to appointing a Development Officer charged with 'creating' the final Trail later that same year. It is likely that the route will not be finally designated until 1995 or 1997. In the interim, the route as described here will remain the 'official' path, with possible minor variations as noted above. When the National Trail comes into existence, it will probably be very similar to the route described in this guide. Early indications are that changes will be few and will not alter the route by more than a couple of kilometres. The CCW will concentrate on taking the route off roads, perhaps giving priority to the section going east from Machynlleth. It would be easy to complain about the sections of road walking that currently link the country walking, but in practice they are quiet sections and do not detract from the interest of a well-thought-out route.

The waymarking on the route, by blue or yellow arrows, varies from good to almost non-existent, and it would be foolhardy to embark on the route without the appropriate Ordnance Survey maps. (The maps given in this book are for guidance only and may not be totally infallible. The maps are marked every 5 kilometres, which approximates to one hour's walking.) The required OS Landranger Sheets are:

Sheet 148   Presteigne and Hay-on-Wye
Sheet 136   Newtown and Llanidloes
Sheet 135   Aberystwyth
Sheet 125   Bala and Lake Vyrnwy

Sheet 126   Shrewsbury

In many areas the OS Pathfinder series are much more useful. The following are required to cover the route:

SO27/37
SO07/17
SO08/18
SO88/98
SO89/99
SH70/SN79
Outdoor Leisure Sheet 23
SH80/90
SJ02/12
SJ01/11
SJ00/10
SJ20/30

THE COUNTRY CODE

The Code was prepared by the Countryside Commission with the help and advice of the many organizations concerned with the welfare of the countryside.

Enjoy the country and respect its life and work.
Guard against all risk of fire.
Fasten all gates.
Keep dogs under close control.
Keep to public footpaths across all farmland.
Use gates and stiles to cross field boundaries.
Leave all livestock, machinery and crops alone.
Take your litter home.
Help to keep all water clean.
Protect wildlife, plants and trees.
Make no unnecessary noise.

THE CELTS IN WALES

In common with the rest of Britain, Wales has been inhabited spasmodically for perhaps a quarter of a million years. Settlement has not been continuous, however, for the population moved south periodically to escape the Ice Ages.

When the ice finally retreated, peoples of the Neolithic cultures occupied the coastal plain of Wales and Anglesey, leaving the upland central dome alone; they did not have the technology either to tame its wilderness or to survive its climate. Later prehistoric cultures did colonize the central area, making occasional use of the high land for ceremonial purposes. The route described in this book visits a burial site of the later Bronze Age, its barrows perched on a spur of the high plateau so that they dominate the surrounding countryside. It also passes close to a stone circle, one of those most enigmatic of sites, also associated with the earliest metal-using peoples.

In central Europe, now known as the Celtic cradle because the two early or proto-Celtic peoples are named after representative sites in that area – Hallstatt in Austria and La Tène in Switzerland – the Bronze Age slowly gave way to the Iron Age. The change was gradual; at first there were a few iron implements, later more and then finally all tools were made of iron. It is likely that the Bronze Age folk were not wiped out by a sudden influx of iron users, but that there was an evolution to an iron-using culture, perhaps with the integration of some external peoples.

In Wales the same thing appears to have happened. In South Wales a site has revealed contemporary bronze and iron objects, and the fairy story of the lady of Llyn y Fan Fach in the Brecon Beacons National Park has strong overtones of the meeting of two cultures without the conquest of one by the other. The story tells of Rhiwallon, a local shepherd who regularly took his lambs to the pasture beside the lake. One day he saw a beautiful girl emerge from the water and sit on a rock at the lake's edge. Rhiwallon fell in love with her and offered her some of his lunch – freshly baked bread. She refused it, and refused unbaked bread when he saw her again next day. Finally, Rhiwallon's mother baked a special form of bread that the girl accepted. The girl then accepted the young shepherd's offer of marriage but only on condition that her father gave consent. She also told Rhiwallon that if he struck her three times she would leave him. Next day, Rhiwallon was staggered to find six identical girls at the lake's edge, the father having five daughters besides the shepherd's love. The father said that Rhiwallon had to identify the correct girl if he was to marry her. The shepherd was perplexed but his love twitched a finger, or toe, so he could recognize her.

The pair were married and lived happily together raising three sons but, in time, Rhiwallon did strike her three times. They were taps rather than blows, the result of incorrect behaviour, as Rhiwallon saw it: the girl laughing at a funeral and crying at a wedding. The girl returned to the lake after the third occasion but often came to see her sons, teaching them the secrets of herbal medicine so that they became great healers. They were the first of the Physicians of Myddfai, a line of doctors from this tiny village close to Llyn y Fan Fach, that stretched down to medieval times.

In some versions of the story, Rhiwallon must not strike the girl with iron rather than his hand, and this, and other aspects, have led many to believe it is a folk memory of the meeting of Iron Age and Bronze Age cultures. All the standard elements are there: food taboos, the girl only eats one form of bread (unleavened?); all foreigners look the same; and the older folk know a great deal about natural remedies. If that is so, then it points to an assimilation of cultures, rather than a conquest.

However, while the iron cultures may have been integrated into the existing Bronze Age system, the country (and at this time, that includes Britain rather than just Wales) became dominated by the Celtic peoples of central Europe. This domination was reinforced by many subsequent invasions or resettlements. The early newcomers could have been settlers in search of new lands, or possibly refugees escaping from the invasions of southerly warlike tribes. Later newcomers were definitely tribes on the run from the Romans who were advancing northward in search of security for Rome's northern border, lands to exploit and people to tax.

The Romans gave the people the name by which they are now known, using Keltoi as their general term, which was interchangeable with Galli for the inhabitants of Gaul (France). It is from the Romans that we gain our first picture of the Celts, who had no written language and therefore have no written history. The Romans were unimpressed. True, the Celts were good in battle, but they were savages – their leaders forever having their praises sung by paid sycophants and their priestly cult a murderous bunch of pagans. To learn of a people's positive qualities there is no point asking their enemies, and the Romans would have been unusual had they wanted to portray the Celts in anything other than a poor light. That said, and with due allowance for consequent distortion, the Roman criticisms are founded on truth – as they saw it. The Celts were indeed a warlike, savage people whose culture – as seen in Wales – seems to have thrived on, almost depended upon, tribal warfare. The tribal leaders did have a stock of bards singing their praises but, in the absence of a written language, oral tradition was the only way of keeping in touch with the past. Moreover, in a military society the need to maintain a ruling elite necessitates enthusiasm for the warrior qualities of the leaders and their ancestors. As for the druids, the Celtic priesthood, no evidence for blood sacrifice exists other than that offered by the Romans, and even if they did practise such sacrifice they were not alone in doing so. Two thousand years ago, the Celts were as much children of their times as we are of our own today, and ours is hardly a bloodless society. Recently it has become fashionable to assign all manner of ancient wisdom to megalith builders and the druids; it may well be that they were more in tune with their environment than we are, but as for being in touch with a higher plane . . . when cornered by the Romans in Anglesey they cursed the advancing legionaries in ritual fashion! It was ancient wisdom against the short sword. There was no contest.

The Romans had arrived in Britain in AD 43 to find a tribal system fully established, similar to those they had already encountered in mainland Europe. Indeed, their knowledge of the Celts which they had acquired in Europe assisted them in their conquest. The Celtic tribes fought each other continually, in an endless series of battles between alliances which formed and reformed as personalities rose and fell in their respective hierarchies. Any king who managed by means fair or foul to create any semblance of order or unity, had his work undone the moment he died. This was inevitable as gavelkind was the custom in the Celtic tribes, the lands of the father being divided equally between the sons. As soon as this happened the sons would fight each other or else another tribe, seeing its chance to rise up the ladder, would overthrown one or other son. Very rarely were the Celts able to unite to resist an outside power, and then only presented a short-term united front.

Prior to the Roman invasion Britain was split up into a number of tribal holdings, but the one which prompted the invasion and offered the stiffest opposition was that of Cunobelinus, the Cymbeline of Shakespeare's play. In AD 40 King Cunobelinus banished his son, Amminius. Why is not certain but it was probably for plotting rebellion, and Amminius went to Rome for help against his family. By the time Aulus Plautius arrived with his army, Cunobelinus was dead and the opposing army was led by two other sons, Togodumnus and Caratacus. Togodumnus was killed early in the campaign but Caratacus stoutly resisted the invaders – suffering defeat after defeat but always rising to resist again a little further to the west. In what is now Wales but was then merely another part of the Celtic homeland, Caratacus stirred the Silures of the south and the Ordovices of the north to join him to throw back the Romans. Around AD 51 there was a final battle – the exact site is unknown but it was in central Wales near the

Shropshire border – and Caratacus was captured. The Romans must have been somewhat dismayed when the Celtic leader escaped and fled north to raise another army. The Brigantes there may well have helped him, but their queen Cartimandua – either pro-Roman already or sensing which way the wind was blowing – handed him over to the Romans. She received her reward from them, even if she did not receive the enthusiastic support of her people, and Caractacus was sent in chains to Rome. There he was paraded as a captive savage and is reputed to have lectured the Roman senate on their idiotic attitude towards those who opposed them: 'If you want to rule the world, does it follow that everyone else welcomes enslavement . . . Spare me, and I shall be an everlasting token of your mercy.' The Romans were impressed by this noble savage and, although he was held until his death, Caratacus lived in honourable captivity. In Wales he was enthusiastically taken up as a hero. After all, he was Celtic, even if he did have the misfortune to have been born near London. Wales is full of references to him, usually as Caradog – the Welsh form of his name – and there are many Caer Caradogs in the area in which the last battle was reputedly fought. The attitude towards this honorary Welshman is typical of their later history. Welshness was an attitude of mind, not a question of birth, though it is now more difficult to join the ranks than previously. Most of the south Wales valley folk emigrated from the Midlands only a few generations ago, and Lloyd George was born in Manchester. This adoption of those who have performed in or for Wales is borne out by the case of Boudicca who has never been truly claimed by the Welsh despite having a pedigree almost identical to that of Caratacus. But her campaigning, which led not to honourable captivity but to death around AD 64, was wholly in 'England'.

Following the subjugation of the Welsh tribes, Wales – as with the rest of Britain as far as Hadrian's Wall – settled down to a long period of Romanized living. This came to an end when the Romans departed in the first quarter of the fifth century, no longer able to police and safeguard this far corner of their Empire from Irish and Pictish raiders. What followed immediately upon their departure was astonishing.

Britain had lived through nearly four centuries of Roman domination, yet virtually as the last Romans legionary shook the British dust from his sandal and went aboard ship, the ancient tribes were regrouping around new kings all of whom could trace their line back to pre-Roman times. The bards returned to sing of ancestral deeds: the Celts had returned to the land!

However, while it is to their credit that the Celts had maintained their culture in the face of occupation, it is sad that they had learned so little from the Romans. Britain had been occupied by a people with one name but a multitude of backgrounds. The Hard Knott fort for example, perhaps the furthest-flung bastion in the whole Roman Empire, buried deep in the hills of the Lake District, had been built by troops from the Yugoslavian Dalmatian coast. What the Romans had taught their subject powers was that unity was all. In *The Once and Future King*, T. H. White's Merlin says: 'I could never stomach these nationalists. If you keep on dividing you end up as a collection of monkeys throwing nuts at each other.' Though written many centuries later as dialogue for another time, the sentiments were as appropriate in fifth-century Britain as at any other period.

Around 450 Vortigern, a Celtic king, was troubled by typical tribal pressures and asked the Saxons of Europe to come to his aid. They came, helped and stayed. Later Vortigern fled to Wales to avoid the new peril he had imported.

Once in Britain the Saxons pushed steadily westward, exploiting this tribal-conflict weakness of the Celts, stopping or retreating occasionally when the Celts fought back and then marching west again. In 577 Cuthwine and Ceawlin fought and killed three Celtic kings – Conmail, Condidan and Farinmail – at the battle of Dyrham just outside Bristol, thus thrusting a Saxon wedge between the Britons of Wales and northern England and those of south-west England. The latter were pushed westward and became the Cornish, maintaining until very recently a language with great similarities to the British languages of Wales and Brittany. Forty years passed and Aethelfrith of Northumbria won a bloody battle at Chester, defeating an army led by a grandson of Brochfael Ysgithrog (Brochfael the Fanged) a feared leader whose coat of arms had been three severed heads. After the battle, Aethelfrith slaughtered thousands of monks, claiming that by praying for a Celtic victory they had fought as much as those who had held swords. This decisive victory cut off the Celts of Wales from those of the Lake counties. Cymru had been formed. That name is in fact Celtic, the people feeling a common bond if not actually acting in unity, and referring to themselves as Cymry, 'fellow countryman'. The name Wales is Saxon: Wallas means 'foreigners'. It has a common root with Valais in Switzerland, Walloon in Belgium and Vlach in Romania.

At the borders of Wales the Saxons stopped, more or less at the border which still separates Wales from England, though this is hardly surprising since the line roughly follows the dyke built by the Saxon King Offa to stop incursions from the Welsh into his kingdom. At first sight this appears ridiculous since it was the Saxons who overran the British Celts, but the Saxons had flinched from the difficulties of fighting in upland Wales and therefore did no more than mount punitive expeditions. A power struggle between rival Saxon earls then relieved the pressure on the Welsh, allowing them to mount raids that were short and bloody and followed by a quick dash back to the safety of the hills. Offa's Dyke put an end to all that.

West of the dyke a number of kingdoms had been rapidly established when the Romans departed and, with changing borders due to the ebb and flow of rival kings, they remained approximately the same for nearly a thousand years. Gwynedd held the lands of what is now the Snowdonia National Park – roughly equivalent to modern Gwynedd – and the granary of Anglesey, making up a readily defensible and highly self-sufficient kingdom. In Wales as a whole Gwynedd invariably held power, or its balance. To the east of Gwynedd lay Powys, while to the south-west were the small kingdoms of Ceredigion, Dyfed and Ystrad Tywi occasionally unified as Deheubarth. In the south-west were Brycheiniog and Buellt and below them Morgannwg and Gwent. It is an interesting fact that the new county names of Wales have marked a return to those of the old kingdoms. Since the districts have maintained the old names – thus preserving the beauty of one such as Merioneth – and introduced a district of Glyndwr, it is difficult to criticize the change on aesthetic grounds.

The kings of Gwynedd commence – in any plausible form that is, since bardic tradition usually pushed a ruler's ancestry back towards the Creation – with Cunedda, known as Wledig ('the Burner'), who lived in the early fifth century. In the Welsh language the king's name would have been pronounced Kin-Etha and it is interesting to speculate whether, heard by non-Welsh speaking Saxons, this could have been translated as King Arthur, the legendary leader of the British against the Saxons. If indeed he did exist, he also lived in the fifth century, although he is usually placed at the end of the century rather than the beginning. Cunedda was followed by Cadwallon, the first of many kings whose name takes the prefix 'cad' meaning 'battle'. After Cadwallon came Maelgwn Gwynedd, and at this point history begins to deal with real people rather than misty figures. Maelgwn was 'the Dragon', a man of huge physical stature and an apparently limitless capacity for violence. As was usual though, he was beloved of the bards and hard, but not cruel, to his subjects. It is with Maelgwn too that we reach those other architects of the Welsh nation, the Celtic Christian saints. Maelgwn gave land to Curig, an Irish missionary, for the creation of a *llan* – a sacred spot where the holy man and his followers lived. Not surprisingly, the land was at Llangurig beside the Wye, on the edge of Plynlimon, and, as even the most cursory glance at a Welsh map shows, Wales is littered with many other *llans* to numerous saints. St David, Dewi Sant, was active about forty years later.

Curig and Maelgwn would have made a strange pair: the one a former soldier turned saint; the other a soldier in every need of his path to heaven being smoothed. In AD 547 Maelgwn 'beheld the Yellow Plague through the Keyhole of the church door and forthwith died'.

These early kings ruled a land which had changed little throughout many centuries for, despite the Saxon horde, there were few refugees in Wales, and the kingdoms were untouched by the invader's hand. And so they continued, behind their dyke, in the endless round of civil war and tribal strife, until the rise of Rhodri Mawr, Rhodri the Great, in the mid-ninth century. It is doubtful whether any previous king had succeeded in unifying the country, and although Rhodri himself did not achieve this either, at least he showed what could be gained by unity.

Rhodri succeeded his father Merfyn to the kingship of Gwynedd in 844, and assumed leadership of Powys when his uncle died heirless in 854. Next he married Angharad of Ceredigion and succeeded to this kingdom when her brother died in 873. However, he never managed to control the southern kingdoms, and must have rued their absence during his almost continual battles with Danes trying to settle the western coast of Wales. Finally, in 877, he died in battle. His kingdom was divided between his sons and Wales was splintered again.

However, Rhodri's sons did leave one gift for posterity. Intent on augmenting their own riches, they attacked and plundered the southern part of the country. The kings of the smaller states sought help from the English ruler, the mighty Alfred, and in return for agreeing to become vassals of the English crown they received his protection. Alfred attacked the north and though he lost the battle of Conwy it was obvious to Rhodri's sons that they could not hope to win or even to survive a war with the English. They too therefore became vassals, thus giving England a legal claim on the whole of Wales. Once again the Welsh flair for 'divide and fight' had been their undoing.

In time of peril from stronger neighbours, this vassal status to the English crown was useful to the kings of Wales. But when peace came it was irksome, though never sufficiently so – nor for enough of them simultaneously – for them to combine and throw out the English. As time went on the English, in touch with continental trends and with, by comparison, virtually unlimited resources, became increasingly difficult to remove. While England, in the main at least, presented a united front at the dyke, the Welsh squabbled and fought behind it.

In the first half of the tenth century, Hywel Dda, Hywel the Good, formed the kingdom of Deheubarth and turned his attentions to the power-house of Wales: the north. He took Gwynedd when their king died in battle with England and then took Powys by force. He is remembered for his coding of Welsh law, a coding which lasted until medieval times. The laws gave women property rights – a thousand years ahead of England in that respect. In the law code everything had its value – a good mouser cat was worth a sheep, for example – and all things were defined: gold plate had to be 'as thick as the nail of a ploughman who has been a ploughman for seven years'. Since money was scarce, fines could be paid in cattle. The laws of Hywel Dda were benign, liberal and just, and their application gave the prospect of a unity based on firm justice. However, the progress he had made – using, it must be said, a degree of violence which hardly warrants the name 'Good' even if his laws were excellent in themselves – did not survive his death.

Following Hywel's death, the Welsh kingdoms were in a confused and strife-torn state for almost a century until Gruffydd ap Llywelyn, a descendant of Hywel, finally achieved a united Wales. He entered into a treaty with the border earls of England, marrying Ealdgyth, daughter of Earl Aelfgar. Unfortunately the ambitious Earl Harold Godwinson convinced Edward the Confessor that Gruffydd was plotting an eastward expansion and invaded Wales on the king's behalf. Gruffydd was pursued to Gwynedd, but for once the Snowdonia mountains failed to hold back the invader and Gruffydd was killed. The united Wales was deliberately fragmented – divide and rule. Harold then married Ealdgyth, who thus had the unenviable fate of becoming widowed by battle twice in three years. But when William the Conqueror arrived in England he not only widowed Ealdgyth, he changed the nature of the Welsh relationship to the English.

Prior to the Norman invasion, the English attitude towards the Welsh was very much that of 'live and let live'. Occasionally there was a need to teach them a lesson, usually of their own asking, but Harold's invasion was an isolated and unhappy incident. The Norman Conqueror's attitude was different, however. William needed land with which to reward his followers and Wales was land. Therefore he decided to call up the legal right to Wales and distribute it.

In fact, the Normans did not have an easy time in their intended conquest of Wales. The country may not have had the unity bequeathed to it by Gruffydd ap Llywelyn – the constant civil wars saw to that – but first Rhys ap Tewdwr in south Wales and then Gruffydd ap Cynon in north Wales each achieved a sufficient land base to thwart the Norman invader. In addition, Wales was not best suited to the Norman form of warfare with its emphasis on cavalry. Any invader of Wales needed quality infantry and, above all, the ability to consolidate gains because the Welsh could be very persistent resistance fighters.

Interestingly, William did not enter into a conquest of Wales as a policy decision; he wanted the land but his commitment was lacking. Instead he chose to reward his followers by allowing them to do the invading for him. To achieve this he set up the Marcher lords, knights who owned land on the March – or border – between England and Wales. A lord of the March had a defined eastern border to his land but the western border was his own affair. It was therefore the Marcher lords who pushed the Norman conquest into the Welsh heartland, becoming infamous for their treachery and their brutality. One lord 'slew the Welsh like sheep, conquered them, enslaved them and flayed them with nails of iron'. Not surprisingly the Marcher lords encountered the resistance of Gruffydd ap Cynon and Rhys ap Tewdwr. Their campaigns were local affairs: the families of Clare, de Braose and Mortimer pushing forward, building a castle, winning a skirmish here, losing one there. A remarkable side-effect of this conquest by attrition was that the Normans were drawn into the Welsh style of tribal warfare. Small alliances were formed between Welsh princes (there were no kings now, except the one in London) and Norman lords, and even between the English king and the Welsh against one of the more powerful and belligerent lords. To cement these alliances there were numerous Norman – Welsh marriages and at times it appears that far from the Norman Marcher lords spreading westward, the Welsh were conquering eastward by the back door.

As might be expected, the timing of Norman conquests in Wales was dependent upon the terrain. In south Wales there are a large number of castles, indicative of frequent pushes and frequent successes. By the time Henry I died virtually the whole of south Wales, from Glamorgan to Pembroke, was in Norman hands. With Henry's death in 1135, however, Gruffydd ap Rhys and his son Lord Rhys re-established the kingdom of Deheubarth and pushed the Normans back towards the Severn. At the same time, Owain Gwynedd, son of Gruffydd ap Cynon, pushed the invaders back to Chester, and Madog ap Maredudd and his brother re-established the kingdom of Powys. Things were not the same as before the arrival of the Normans, however. The century of occupation, partial or total, had caused certain areas of Wales to become pro-Norman, if not openly, then certainly covertly. A good example is that of the Flemings of Pembrokeshire who later rose against Owain Glyndwr. This creation of enclaves of 'Englishness' in Wales was to have serious repercussions in later centuries.

Henry II attempted to subdue the new Welsh princedom but was not successful and had to accept the independence of both Owain Gwynedd and Lord Rhys – Lord of Ystrad Tywi, a Norman title, despite its holder being Welsh. Owain died in

1170, Lord Rhys in 1187, Henry in 1189. Typically, the deaths of Owain and Rhys caused internal strife in Wales, but Richard I was unable to take advantage of this because of his virtually continual absence on crusade. King John came to the throne in 1199, but by then Llywelyn ap Iorwerth – a grandson of Owain Gwynedd – had become Prince of Gwynedd. Llywelyn Fawr, Llywelyn the Great, was an astute politician and, by good politics and the occasional exercise of a firm hand, became effective ruler of Wales by 1203. He strengthened his own position by marrying King John's daughter Joan and by siding with the barons in their dispute with the crown which ended in the signing of Magna Carta.

Sadly, the unity that Llywelyn achieved, and which was the only hope that Wales had against the ever-present pressure of the Marcher lords, was lost on his death. His son Dafydd lost control of Powys and Deheubarth and when Dafydd died his nephews Owain and Llywelyn, who succeeded him, saw their principality so fragmented that when the English king invaded – finally using Welsh disunity to advantage – they could do nothing but accept the effective surrender of the Treaty of Woodstock in 1247. Wales was now just another group of lordships answerable to the English crown and, what is more significant, taxable by it.

When in 1255 Llywelyn ap Gruffydd, Llywelyn the Last, finally united Gwynedd the fight that he led against the crown was little more than the rebellion of a Marcher lord. The Welsh, looking to re-establish Welsh independence, did not see it that way but that is how it appeared to the English kings Henry III and Edward I. At first Llywelyn restored to Wales those parts lost in the Treaty of Woodstock; he pushed back the Marcher lords to Cheshire, Shropshire and Hereford-shire in the north, retaking Breconshire in mid-Wales. Significantly, however, he failed to retake south Wales. By 1400 this area would have been 'English' for 150 years. In 1267 the Treaty of Montgomery brought peace and Llywelyn became Prince of Wales. Had he stopped then he might have maintained all he had gained, but he continued to harass the borders of his principality. While old Henry III was king he could hope to avoid crown retribution, but Edward I was different; he invaded Wales, forcing Llywelyn to accept the Treaty of Aberconwy in 1277 which took back many of his gains. Llywelyn was quiet for a time but then in 1282 rose against the king, only to be killed in a skirmish at Cilmery near Builth Wells. A huge monolith marks the spot where the last native Prince of Wales to be recognized as such was killed. Edward I built his 'ring of stone' castles, clamped like a manacle around Gwynedd and Wales, so that the people should remember they were a subject race.

The effect on the Welsh morale was catastrophic:

> Oh God! That the sea might surge up to You, covering
>   the land!
> Why are we left to long-drawn weariness?
> There is no refuge from the terrible Prison.

This was written by a bard in 1283, when not only was Llywelyn dead but his brother Dafydd had been captured and executed. The independence known by the men of Gwynedd and Powys for almost a thousand years, even if they had spent it in petty squabbles, was over.

In one sense Edward's conquest was not catastrophic, as he was a humane man and left the Welsh with their language and culture. The problem was that the country was administered by those who felt that a subject race should know its place – down-trodden and well-taxed. The English never let the Welsh forget that they were Welsh. Eventually it was to surprise them that the Welsh remembered it too.

When Edward gave the Welsh his son as Prince of Wales at Caernarfon in 1301, it was a well-meant gesture which was favourably received, despite the bitter comment it now provokes. In Edward III's French wars the Welsh fought with distinction at Crêcy and Poitiers but at home there was always an undercurrent of resentment. There were frequent minor revolts and the harsh treatment these received only exacerbated the problem. The Marcher lords continued to over-tax the native Welsh, in addition to treating them as serfs in their own country. From 1348 to 1350 Black Death ravaged the land, adding to the torment. North Wales was a poor country agriculturally and the heavy burden of taxes and young men lost to war and disease meant that the Welsh slipped into a form of half-starved slavery for which, not unnaturally, they held the English responsible. The better farming areas of south Wales were able to survive more easily and therefore held less of a grudge. As the fourteenth century drew to a close, the Welsh of the north were as tinder waiting for a spark to ignite rebellion. The south was straw – whether it would prove to be dry or wet straw would depend on circumstances.

The Route

KNIGHTON TO ABBEY CWMHIR

The route that commemorates Owain Glyndwr's name and explores the countryside of mid-Wales starts close to the site of his greatest military success, at Knighton, just a couple of miles north-east of Pilleth.

Knighton is a border market town, associated not only with our walk but also with the Offa's Dyke footpath, for it sits about half-way along that route and is the headquarters of the Association concerned with the pathway. But for all its market town bustle and association with quiet days spent walking the local country, Knighton has a bloody past.

Its position, on high ground controlling the narrowing of the Teme valley which was a gateway to Wales or England, ensured that the town's site was strategically important from the time when the Saxons confronted the Cymry across what is now the border of Wales. Even before then this area may have been of military significance, for Caer Caradoc, three miles away to the north-east, is named for Caratacus, the British leader in the fight against invading Romans. As was once noted, 'The country around is eloquent of war and foray.'

It has been suggested that when Caer Caradoc was occupied there was a smaller look-out fort at Bryn-y-castell a little way east of the town centre. This was Cnwc-din, the fort on the hill spur which became Cneithune, then Kenithtun, then Knytheton and finally Knighton. Since later historians proposed the more obvious 'Knight's town' from Sir Roger Mortimer, a Norman lord, the Welsh purists have favoured Tref-y-Clawdd – shortened to Trefyclo, 'the town on the dyke'. It would be one of life's ironies if a truly Welsh name has been deposed, even despised, in favour of one based on the building programme of an English king.

The early Norman lords at Knighton may have used the Bryn-y-castell site, as indeed may Rhodri Mawr at an earlier date, but when it was raised, the stone-built castle was on a site to the west of the town's centre. This castle was raised by the Mortimers but seems to have been small, perhaps because of the closeness of another castle at nearby Knucklas. Both were constructed at the turn of the twelfth century but neither survived the 1262 campaign of Llywelyn ap Gruffydd. When relative peace returned the Mortimers restored Knighton Castle but it was destroyed again – and this time for good – when Glyndwr came this way in 1402; Owain came from the west and 'there is scarce a house left standing between Llandiloes and Knighton'.

The Mortimers were a powerful Marcher family, with ambitions to be king-makers and, occasionally, kings. Roger Mortimer was exiled to France by Edward II and there lived with Isabella, Edward's queen, and her son, the future Edward III. He formed an army which invaded England in 1326 and won power, capturing Edward. It was probably on Mortimer's instructions that the king was murdered at Berkeley Castle and for a time the Marcher lord was the power in England. Ultimately Edward III recognized the threat posed by Roger's arrogance and he was arrested and executed at Tyburn, near what is now Marble Arch.

The family did not learn any lessons from this and in 1461 another Mortimer, Edward, commanded the Yorkist army at Mortimer's Cross, 16 kilometres to the south-east, where the Lancastrian army was utterly defeated. A Welsh captain of the defeated army was beheaded and his head placed on the steps of Hereford Cathedral, where 'a mad woman combed his hair and washed away the blood from his face, and got candles and set them round his head, all burning, more than a hundred'.

Was she mad or clairvoyant? The man's grandson was to

turn the tables on his grandfather's executioners and to found a dynasty – for the mad woman tended the head of Owen Tudor.

The new peace allowed the Marcher lands to be brought under the proper control of England's government, and while this finally (?) ended Welsh hopes for independence it did bring stability into the lives of the ordinary folk whose misfortune it had been to be born into the area. Knighton was at first placed in the county of Shropshire but transferred to Radnorshire by the Act of Union of 1536; its Norman market charter and position right on the new Welsh–English border ensured its prosperity. In 1854 the market witnessed Radnorshire's last case of wife-selling when a local man led in his wife with a rope around her neck. Another man bid a shilling and the seller was so pleased with the bargain that he threw in the rope as well.

Today Knighton is a picturesque old market town set on the side of a hill, around a clock tower very reminiscent of the one in Machynlleth which marks the half-way point on our route. From the clock tower square the eye is drawn to Kinsley Woods, which lie in England, the modern boundary between the countries forsaking Offa's Dyke and following the Teme. As if to emphasize the Englishness of the wood, trees at its western end have been planted to spell ER in gold against the green mass.

The Welsh inhabitants of Knighton today, shopping in the steeply sloping Tudor 'Narrows', may not be aware that their ancestors would have walked in fear at the same spot. A Welshman caught east of Offa's Dyke had an ear cut off, and the dyke put Knighton in England. The line of the dyke is followed by Offa's Road from the B4355 to the castle site. From the B4355 to the river the dyke runs along Conjuror's Drive, a link with the time not so long ago when this area of Radnorshire was famour for its wizards or conjurors, skilled in the curing of animals and people by spell-casting.

Glyndwr's Way leaves Knighton along the A488 which leads towards Pilleth, skirts the Radnor Forest (an underrated

Welsh upland) and leads on into the Wye Valley and the wilderness of Elenydd. At 275 718 a sign points the way right (west) on to a minor lane. This lane follows the Wilcome Brook back up its pleasant valley, bearing right when another lane goes off to Cwmgilla (269 719), and then left and down at a Y-junction (268 724). The way ahead now is straightforward – climbing Bailey Hill, an extended ridge separating the valleys of the Teme and the Lugg.

To the right of where we emerge on to the road that runs along the ridge (255 727), there was until 1861 a race course on the high flat summit and there is still a Racecourse Farm. The views from the ridge top are excellent both south to the wooded flanks of the Wilcome vale and north to the valley of the Teme. Below us is Knucklas (Cnwclas), the green hill that held another Norman castle.

An earlier castle than the Norman one lay at Felindre, to the north-west and on our route. This was lived in by the son of Uther Pendragon of Crug-y-byddar. Uther's son, Arthur, went to the assistance of two brothers, freeing them from their imprisonment by giants. The boys' father, Gogfran Gawr, himself a giant from Brecon, was so thrilled that he offered Arthur his daughter, Gwynhwyfar, in marriage. Arthur and Guinevere (the English form of her name) lived in his castle at Knucklas, and it was from there that Arthur set out to free Britain from the Saxons and to found his Round Table of Knights. When in the nineteenth century a great slab was lifted at a mound near Monaughty Poeth, just the other side of the Teme from Knucklas, the excavators found the skeletons of five tall men.

At Knucklas too Vavasour Powell was born. He was the governor of churches in the border region under the Long Parliament which followed the Civil War and a man of strong, sometimes contradictory, opinions who quarrelled with most people in authority at some time. He supported Cromwell, was later imprisoned by him and finally died in Fleet prison after the Restoration.

Knucklas Viaduct

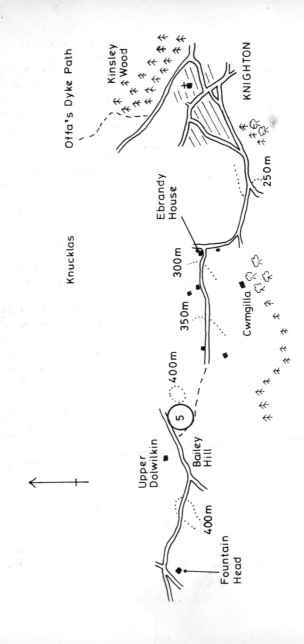

From our standpoint the village, a tiny huddle of buildings, is dominated by the elegant lines of the viaduct carrying the railway into mid-Wales. Stone from the castle site was plundered to build the arches and, as if to make amends, the builders put towers at each end and embattled the parapet.

The route continues along the Bailey Hill lane, eventually trading the views north and south for some more local ones – a solitary tree among the fern, an ancient wind-torn hedge on the skyline, a pond in the middle of nowhere incongruously fed by a piped spring.

A road to Knucklas is passed on the right (230 729) and then as a house – the spring-surrounded Fountain Head – comes into view, a stony track leads off right (westward). To the left of this lane is a large and ancient tumulus where in 1814 a horde of pre-Civil War coins was found, probably buried against the coming strife. The war came and went, but the owner did not return.

A camp sits at the top of Fron-goch, the hill spur pointing towards the River Lugg at Llangunllo. Here, until the first quarter of this century, the collector of a pair of ancient taxes was elected by auction – the lowest offer for the wage required for the job was accepted. There is nothing particularly unusual about that, you may say, since the idea of accepting the lowest tender for collecting taxes or tolls is well-known. But here the auction was held in a slit trench and the final deal was made when all parties concerned joined hands in a hole dug at the end of the trench. Photographs exist of the ceremony – groups of well-dressed, earnest men clasping hands while standing waist-deep in a hole, surrounded by equally well-dressed and earnest spectators. They look like stills from a surreal comedy sketch. And as if that was not enough, the ground where it all took place is known as the Holy Piece, from holey piece!

Our route traverses around above Fron-goch, gently descending and then levelling out as it swings northward. It is a green lane when it drops westward towards Llancoch, a 'hamlet' with virtually no houses beside the mid-Wales railway.

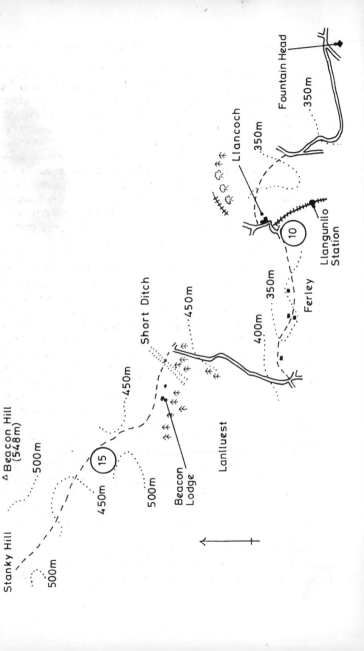

Close to Llancoch is a rail halt, named for Llangunllo, a kilometre or so south. In this part of Wales it is common for the halts to be well-separated from their named towns or villages; the Llanbister Road Halt, for example, is 3 kilometres west of Llangunllo, above 8 kilometres from Llanbister itself. The stations are a long way from the villages but, as every schoolboy knows, they are close to the lines . . .

Turn left at the minor road (207 738) and follow it across the opening of a railway tunnel to a grass triangle at 206 735. Here blue arrows on telegraph pole and tree point the way towards Ferley and the first piece of 'rough' walking. Ferley is from the Welsh *fferllyd*, meaning 'cold' in the sense of exposed to the elements, which is an appropriate description.

Beyond Ferley the track northward at 188 734 is followed to the ancient, heather-covered rampart of Short Ditch. The name is apt, the structure being only a few hundred yards long. It is said to be the remains of a defence thrown up in 1402 by Edmund Mortimer to protect Knighton from Owain Glyndwr. If that is true, then it is astonishing! The ditch is about 10 kilometres from Knighton; if a circular defence was planned it would have been 65 kilometres around, and it would have needed to be continuous or else Glyndwr would simply have gone round behind it. The manpower required to complete and man such a defence would have been colossal. Perhaps Mortimer anticipated a mountain-route advance, or perhaps there is another explanation.

Beyond Short Ditch we break out on to open hill, the heather-topped and leg-wearing flanks of Pool and Stanky Hills, and Black Mountain. When the bridle-paths end, the walking is rough and the waymarking non-existent, but the views and air are good and escape to the salvation of an exposed lane is easy to the west. On the other side of Pool Hill from our route, the Lugg rises in a wilderness of heather to flow down past Pilleth.

Beyond Black Mountain – though the lowest of the three peaks we have passed, it is the one mountain among hills – there are a few tracks at the head of the Warren Brook valley,

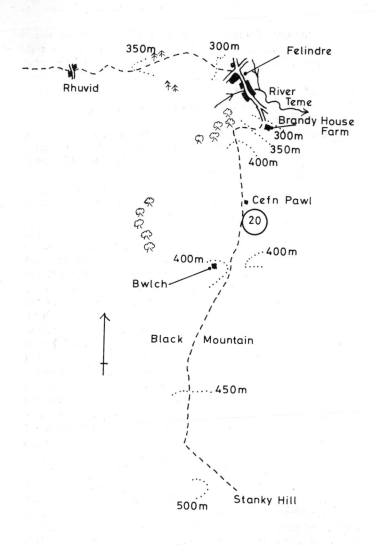

and we join one of these at Cefn Pawl (169 796). This is at the end of a long lane from Beguildy, birthplace of Ieuan Ddu or Black Jack, a famous local conjuror. As Dr John Dee he became Elizabeth I's tutor, a man respected at court an eminent mathematician – as well as astrologer – of his day. It is likely that Shakespeare used this Radnor wizard as the model for Prospero.

Beyond Cefn Pawl a pathway continues northward, skirting the hill to reach the edge of Mill Wood. Follow the wood edge and then go east to Brandy House farm (172 807). Go down the farm lane to the road, and turn left into Felindre.

There is an inn at Felindre but little else, and the village is left by following the green lane westward (right) at Upper House farm, reached by turning left after the inn.

Two paths leave Upper House farm, ours being the lane which goes right beyond the farm and up the ridge spur to the woodland above Crug-y-byddar. Two mounds here, on opposite banks of the River Teme, are the legendary home of Uther Pendragon, Arthur's father. 'Pendragon' means 'dragon's head', 'dragon' being used to distinguish this warlord from others who had different wild-beast names. Some have suggested that here is the origin of the Welsh dragon symbol.

Beyond the wood above the Teme is Rhuvid (148 813) from which a track leads westward, gently climbing the Rhuvid Bank to Hope's Castle farm (132 817). From here the views are wonderful and remain so as the lane we join drops down to cross the Gwenlas brook. Just after the brook, take a path left that goes west of Fiddler's Green farm (117 816), taking a short cut to the tumuli at 112 822. As these Bronze Age round barrows were placed at the top of the northern end of a high ridge of land, Rhiw Porthnant, the view is expansive. This area of Radnorshire is strangely neglected by the tourist but can boast scenery as fine – though clearly not as mountainous – as any that exists north or south. Those who brought their dead here wished to erect a monument which would make an impact on the landscape and would perhaps allow the spirits of the dead to remain in touch with their country. They succeeded.

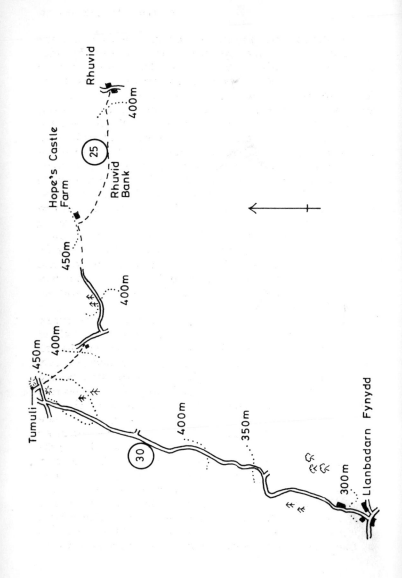

Rhuvid

400m

Hope's Castle
Farm

25

Rhuvid
Bank

450m

400m

400m

450m

400m

Tumuli

450m

30

400m

350m

300m

Llanbadarn Fynydd

From the barrows turn left and left again at the crossroads (110 820), to follow the road down into Llanbadarn Fynydd. Research earlier this century suggested that two stories from the *Mabinogion* could be fairly accurately placed in this area of Radnorshire, and an extension of this research suggested that some of the campaigns fought by Arthur against the Saxons could also be associated with the same place. It has even been suggested that Llanbadarn could be the site of Mons Badoni-cus, Mount Badon, where Arthur fought the twelfth battle – the last and greatest – of his campaign against the Saxons. There is no evidence anywhere in Britain for the true battle site, though there are projected sites from Scotland to Dorset, the currently favoured one being on the Ridgeway path in Wiltshire. On the basis of the name alone, Badon, there are countless potential sites, but Llanbadarn is not one of these since its name is clearly from *llan*, the normal 'church' prefix of many Welsh names, and Padarn, the sixth-century disciple of David. The second word added to the name is a mutation of *mynydd* meaning 'hill', for Padarn's church here was set among the hills.

However, if Arthur had fought at Badon he would surely have made his castle – if not his battlefield – the conical hill three kilometres south of Llanbadarn on which sits Castell Dinboeth. The name is a Welsh corruption of Maud's castle, for it was named for Roger Mortimer's widow after he had built it in the thirteenth century. Though the site bears a thirteenth-century Norman name, it had a long Welsh pedigree before that and there is evidence of a very ancient hill-fort. The site is easily approached by a path that forces an Alpine-style way up the road embankment from 090 751; the hillside is impressively steep, the inhabitants of the castle on its flat top paying for their security with a stiff approach climb. On the summit the remains are poor yet impressive. There is a rock-ditch, littered with the stones of long-gone walls, and a single chunk of thick wall, shaped like the Old Man of Hoy, high above it. The final destruction is thought to have been by Llywelyn ap Gruffydd. The views are impressive: to the east the hills we have traversed – virtually the whole of our route – are laid out; to the west the route forward can be discerned. South and north, along the Ithon valley, the view is no less impressive. It is a wonderful spot.

Since we have ventured from our route, let us go a little way further, still southward. At Llanano church (096 744) there is arguably the finest rood screen in Wales. It dates from the turn of the sixteenth century and is a beautifully executed and inventive background with niches containing figures of Christ, the apostles and prophets. The figures are late nineteenth-century replacements, and I love the way that some of the prophets wear sashes with their names on, like modern beauty queens.

South again at Llanbister is another fine church. The beauty here lies in the way that successive architects have used the hilly site to add interest to the building – it is a maze of levels and steps. There are steps up in the porch, and again inside to the level of the nave; then more steps to the ancient gallery and steps down to an unusual feature: a baptistry for total immersion.

In addition, both churches are well-sited: Llananno beside the Ithon, Llanbister on its hill. Llanbadarn church is also well set beside the Ithon and we pass it on our journey west. The lane crosses the Ithon and continues around a long, tight left-hand bend to a crossroads. Here turn right (westward) up a stony track – *not* hard right and back down a green lane – and follow this to where it ends on the flank of Garn Hill. Now go around the head of the shallow valley to the south to the col (076 774) between Castle Bank and Moel-dod. Here the route turns south, skirting (or climbing) Moel-dod and going over Yr Allt to Ty'n-y-pant (084 751). During the last stages of this section, Castell Dinboeth dominates the view eastward. Take the farm lane to the road.

At the road the route is signposted soutwards to Bwlch farm (085 748). At Bwlch go south, not on along the lane to

The rood screen Llanano church

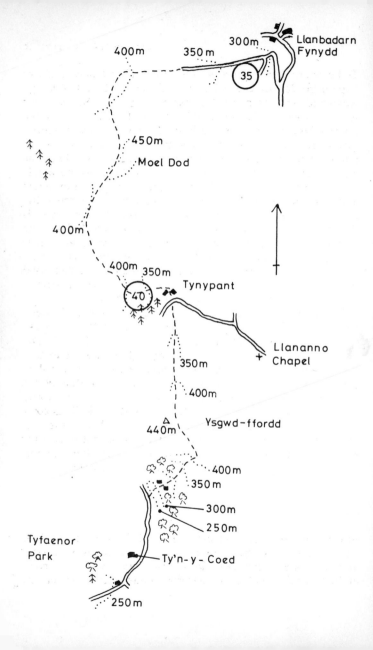

Treboeth, to climb up towards the triangulated summit above Ysgwd-ffordd. At the col south of this peak (088 748), go westward, steeply down to, and through, the Neuadd-fach woods, over the Bachell brook and on to the road. At the point where the road is reached, do not miss the beautiful rowan tree, red-ladened in the autumn – as with the descent into the Bachell valley itself, it is as splendid as anything of its kind. This valley is one of the finest stretches on the whole route, exemplifying that Wales is not only rugged mountains and exposed moorland. We shall experience that too – the former near Plynlimon, the latter at Nant-yr-Eira – but here is the soft, green wooded Wales. Our route now follows the minor road down the valley, past superb trees and river views, the ruin of an old shed and a little bridge. It is as good a mile as we shall walk, so savour it. And do not be disturbed that it is a tarmac path we follow. It is not of tarmac the walker complains but of cars – and you see few of those.

The lane passes through an avenue of rowan and hazel, hawthorn and sloe to Ty-Faenor (071 711), the Manor House built with stone from Abbey Cwmhir. Beyond is a gate; immediately past that, turn right through another gate to a lane. Take care here to follow a route parallel to the valley, passing Bryn-moel (073 713) and on to Abbey Cwmhir, as it is relatively easy to be seduced on to a lane heading north into the impenetrable woodland of Cwmcynydd Bank. This comment is based on experience – despite map and compass etc., I went north and on and on for reasons I cannot even now explain. And one tree soon looked very much like another. But of course, not everybody will be as daft as I was!

ABBEY CWMHIR TO LLANIDLOES

Abbey Cwmhir should be one of the high spots of the walk. It was built for Cistercian monks, an order founded at Citeaux in France by St Robert of Molesmes on the feast of St Benedict in 1098. Each abbot of a Cistercian house made an annual

pilgrimage to Cîteaux and this, with the Cistercians' love for solitude, has led to some quite superb buildings, beautifully sited. Think of Fountains and Rievaulx and of this spot in the quiet Clywedog valley.

Cwmhir was founded in 1143, but this was a short-lived venture and it was re-founded by one Cadwallon ap Madoc, a cousin of Rhys ap Gruffydd, Prince of South Wales, in 1176. Some stories tell of a joint founding with Roger Mortimer and William Fitzalan, two Norman Marcher lords. This would seem strange, as the March lands were subject to almost continuous bickering between the Welsh and their new neighbours at that time. The Norman lords were, however, a very pious breed and the simple dignity of the sheep-farming Cistercians would certainly have appealed to the Welsh. Perhaps the site's remoteness and its spirituality allowed it to become a symbol of peace to both sides. The son and grandson of Cadwallon also endowed the abbey, whose monks had come from the mother church of Whitland. Some idea of the strange times in which the abbey grew up, and of the strange bedfellows the co-founders made – if indeed they were co-founders – is evidenced by the fact that Cadwallon's son Hywel, after endowing the abbey with extra land, was executed at Bridgnorth in 1212 for the murder of a Norman lord. Later, in 1231, the abbey may have become involved in the feud between Llywelyn the Great and Henry III. I say 'may', because the true casualty of Henry's action has not been reliably identified. Henry was at Hereford with his army, preparing to pursue Llywelyn who was near Montgomery Castle. It is said that Llywelyn persuaded an abbot to tell some of Henry's men that he knew of the prince's position. These men, convinced that they had caught Llywelyn off-guard and with only a small band of men, hurried on horseback to the site but became trapped in the treacherous quagmire of a water meadow and were slaughtered. The outraged Henry plundered and burnt the abbot's grange and

On the Way near Treboeth

fired the abbey. But which abbey? The story talks of Cumira, but is that Cwmhir, or Cymer near Dolgellau? Cwmhir is 40 kilometres from Montgomery and about 65 kilometres from Hereford, while Cymer is 55 kilometres and 160 kilometres respectively. On distance alone it seems that if the story has any truth at all, it is more likely to be centred around Cwmhir. Certainly there is architectural evidence that one period of building ceased around 1230. Some restoration probably took place, as it did again after Glyndwr destroyed the abbey in 1401. The reasons for that destruction are not well understood. It is said that Owain believed the English monks of Cwmhir to be spies. How ironic if true – destroyed by an English king for suspected help given to a Welsh prince, and by a Welsh prince for suspected help given to an English king.

What was it that they destroyed? Leland, the early six-teenth-century travel writer, said of Cwmhir that 'no church in Wales is seen of such length as the foundations of the walls there begun doth show, but the third part of the work was never finished'. Of the projected work only the nave was completed, and that was 74 metres long, an enormous length approached by no other Cistercian abbey and by very few minsters and cathedrals. The existing marked out base area is 78 metres by 22 metres.

The nave was constructed with fourteen arched bays, four more than exist at Wells Cathedral and, according to expert judgement, equalling Canterbury in their splendour as a colonnade in Early English design. The abbey was built for sixty monks: despite its endowments, it was never a wealthy abbey but maintained the austerity sought by its Order's founding monks but forgotten by many English abbeys. When the Dissolution came, in 1536, there were only three monks and the abbey and its lands were valued at £24 19s 4d. The abbey building passed at one remove to the Fowlers, a rich local family, and one of their descendants built Ty-Faenor with abbey stone. It was usual for the first owner after Dissolution to strip out any roof lead, a process which started a decay that was hastened by the use of the site as a local

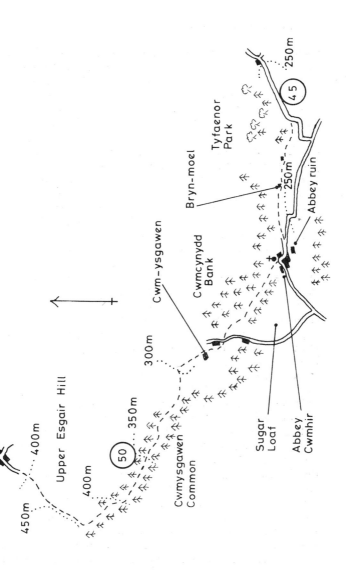

quarry for good-quality dressed stone. At Cwmhir we can be grateful for one profound departure from this norm for, although the abbey itself was plundered (even the Hall opposite the site is of abbey stones and it was not built until the 1830s, five of the nave bays were used in the reconstruction of Llanidloes church in 1542. The stones were not properly labelled and are not therefore in perfect original form, and one bay had to be narrowed because somebody could not handle a measuring stick properly, but the glory is still there to see. Imagine what a double row of fourteen bays would have looked like. Three times the length of the Llanidloes nave!

As I have said, these ruins should be one of the highlights of the trip – but they are not. In 1282 Llywelyn the Last died in a skirmish near Brecon and the English king he had defied barbarously cut off the Welsh prince's head to exhibit it in a freak show in London. But what of the body? The monastic chronicles of Worcester and Chester – widely separate places – and much oral tradition has it that the body was brought here to Cwmhir and that in the church the last true-born Prince of Wales (Glyndwr could trace a lineage to the Royal houses but was not true-born) was buried. No gravestone for Llywelyn has ever been found, no headless body has ever been unearthed, but it seems likely that he is here. Today, at the right time of year, the ruins are a caravan site and the stone is still open to the casual plunderer. It is ironic that the Welsh, so proud of their history and of the echoes of their independent past, should allow this hallowed spot to fall into disrepair. More than an irony, it is a shame.

Today the visitor to Abbey Cwmhir who knows nothing of the ruins sees the beauty and experiences the peace of the Clywedog valley, and notices the inn sign and the new church. Unless he knows of it, he misses the ruins of the Abbey of the Blessed Virgin Mary altogether.

The inn is the Happy Union and the sign depicts a man

On the Way near Abbey Cwmhir

with a leek in his hat riding on a goat. The church is opposite the inn, an unusual design from the middle of the last century; the spire is curious, octagonal with wooden slats almost like a dovecote, and supports an incongruous though pleasing flourish of plant life.

From the village our route continues along the Monk's Way, an ancient pathway that linked Cwmhir to the Abbey of Strata Florida, near Pontrhydfendigaid. That walk, crossing the beautiful wilderness of Elenydd between the Elan and Claerwen reservoirs, is worthwhile but its exploration is another story.

The Monk's Way is joined opposite the Happy Union Inn, beside the lonely petrol pump, and is followed through the woodland to the minor road at 045 719. Here the wayfarer meets what is probably the first ambiguous metal signpost for Glyndwr's Way. Whether by poor design – the use of a round pole allowing the wind to shift the sign – or by some local humorist, there is a tendency for the metal signs on the route to point the wrong way. I have passed this sign many times and usually it points right, but the route goes left and *then* right by the commemorative tree and fights its way behind the houses to Cwm-y-sgaw (042 721) and the forest track at 041 724. I say 'fight' because the path is not well-defined. It is probably easier to go right and to follow the road to the lane (043 726) after Fishpool farm, then to turn left (westward) along it and to continue into the forest.

Beyond the forest, at 020 735 on the summit of the highest local peak, is Castell-y-garn, a burial chamber which contained a stone chest full of human bones. It is one of many such burial mounds in the area and there are also standing stones and a stone circle. Apparently this was an important part of Wales to the first metal-using folk of the Bronze Age. It is food for thought that they too might have appreciated its scenic beauty – would they now recognize the view, with its strange clumping of alien trees?

Abbey Cwmhir church

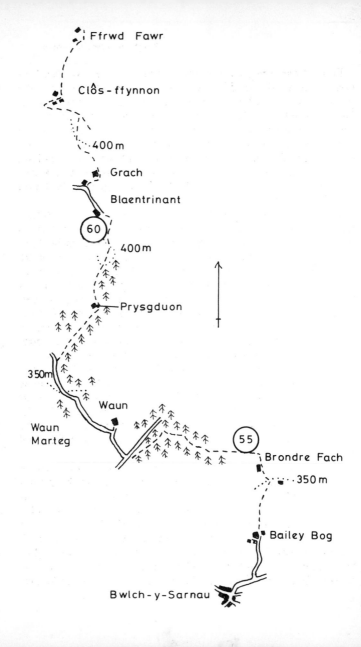

From Castell-y-garn the route drops down to Bwlch-y-sarnau, a small windswept hamlet named for its col-like position where paths met as they crossed the wild moorland. Beyond the hamlet there is a really fine piece of country, not pretty in the sense of Cwmhir, nor wild in the sense of the high moor, but a combination of the two. There are trees, but they are pinched by the wind and the fields have a bleak look about them. It is a strangely beautiful, twilight land and with it comes the first view of high Wales, the ranges of Plynlimon and Cadair Idris beyond the Severn's source.

The route leaves Bwlch-y-sarnau by road to Llaithddu, going north-east to 0933 748, where a signposted track leads down off the ridge followed by the road. This track leads to the inelegantly named Baily Bog (034 753) and on to Brondre Fach (034 762). From there a track leads to a forestry road through the Waunmarteg plantation, going left at a T-junction (020 767) and down to the 'main' road at its elbow (017 763). Over the last stage of this walk the 'sterile' forest offers up some real gems for the walker. Do not miss the drainage channels at its edge which have been converted into long, thin ponds. Or the real pond to the left at the wood exit.

Turn right (north-west) and follow the lane towards a continuation of the plantation, beyond which the route is signed right (north-east) at 007 774. Follow the straightforward track to Prysgduon (013 782) and on to Blaentrinant (013 792). It is at this stage that the view north-east opens up, as the route contours around the scarp-like edge of Rhyddhywel plateau.

Beyond Blaentrinant the route takes a devious meandering way, north to Grach farm (013 797), north again to the stream (010 805), which is followed and crossed to 007 805. Go right (east), passing Clos-ffynnon (008 806) to the wood edge (011 814). Continue along the edge, then north where the edge bends back left to 011 817, where a track goes left and downhill towards Cwm farm (009 826). Do not go into the farm, but take the path which turns sharply left to follow and cross the stream; follow this down to 002 819. From here the route goes right (northward) to skirt the small conical hill that lies north-west to reach Waen farm (992 822) and the road at 990 820. As an alternative, the wayfarer can continue to the road from 002 819 and turn right to reach the same point.

This is a very pleasant section of the route, with striking views of the Dethenydd mountains, especially in the first stages. It is not the easiest of walking, however, with streams to cross, and it is essential that a map is carried since the route-finding – although straightforward enough – is usually by map rather than by blue arrow. It is fair to say, however, that since the route is contouring around the edge of the high plateau it is easy to escape to the road to the west, and invariably easy to pick out the line ahead.

The route goes right and at 986 819 an unsigned but obvious green lane – opposite a fine holly tree – is taken, between rows of hazel trees, on past Prospect farm to the road at 985 830. The prospect from the farm is a view of the Severn valley and is well worth the name. Despite our proximity to the river, which is now only 3 kilometres away, it is a long way below. Go right at the road and on to Newchapel.

The new chapel was built in 1740 by an amalgamation of Non-conformist faiths, but rapidly became entirely Baptist. Behind us is Old Chapel Hill where, according to the local stationmaster when talking to the Reverend Francis Kilvert, Edward I signed a peace treaty with the Welsh. There is no proof that this is true, but it is an interesting example of the snippets which Kilvert collected into his famous diaries. Kilvert is rightly associated with the Wye Valley, Clyro and Bredwardine, but he also served at the church in St Harmon a few miles south of Newchapel, so there are sections of his diary which deal with this area.

At the chapel the route is signed left (north-west) and is signed again at 983 838, where it leaves the road to drop down to cross the Nant Bradnant in a delightful wooded valley. A lane is joined at 977 838 and this is followed down into Llanidloes, accompanying the Lletty Coch-nant stream on its way to the Severn. The stream is called the red brook, for the water is stained by haematite.

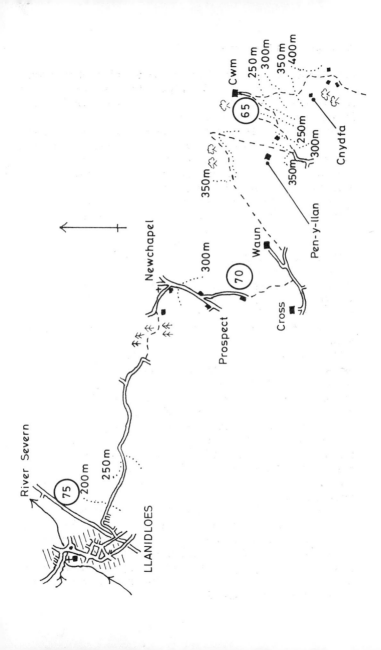

LLANIDLOES TO MACHYNLLETH

At the time of Arthur – that is, in the first half of the sixth century – the land here at the last ford of the Severn was controlled by Llawfrodedd Coch, the Red Knight, who was one of the three herdsmen of the cattle of Mudd Hael, a Celtic god. His grandson Idloes was a famously pious holy man in the early part of the seventh century and, with that eye for an ideal spot which so characterizes the early Celtic saints, he founded his *llan* here on the south bank of the Severn and at the geographical centre of Wales.

There was an early market here and the centre of the town is still the Market Hall. But before that there was, of course, the Norman castle, perpetuated now only in the name of the Mount Inn on the road to Llangurig and the Wye valley. It is to the Market Hall, however, that the tourist – newcomer and *aficionado* alike – returns. It is an elegant structure, timber-framed with one end of stone and the other of brick, and a bell turret complete with bell and weather-vane. The bell used to ring at eight in the evening to tell the tradesmen to close their shops. It has had no clapper for many years now, though it was rung with a poker in 1900 to announce the relief of Mafeking!

The building dates from the late sixteenth century, and is now the oldest timber-framed market hall in Wales, withstanding not only the test of time but also its precarious position in the middle of a busy road. Despite its name, it has had many functions: one end, the crib, was the town jail; it was a courthouse, a meeting-house for Quakers, Wesleyans (John Wesley himself preached outside it, from a stone still existing) and Baptists; it was also library and working men's institute, and a meeting place for local Chartists before their riot in the town. Today it houses a museum of local industry.

The Chartists supported the People's Charter, a six-point

The Market Hall, Llanidloes

plan for electoral reform. Today the points at issue, such as payment of MPs, total franchise, etc. appear commonplace. Five points have been granted and the sixth – annual parliaments – is not taken seriously by any credible party. But in 1839, the idea of the Charter appalled those who controlled the government: it reeked of social justice, the abolition of privilege and other such malodorous reforms. The Chartists were clearly dangerous revolutionaries, to be treated accordingly. In general, the civil strife that accompanied Chartism was most pronounced in working-class areas such as South Wales, where an uprising at Newport led to deaths and transportations, and here at the heart of the Welsh woollen industry. In 1833 there were eighteen fulling mills at the town.

In Llanidloes the Chartists were bitterly opposed by the town mayor, Thomas Marsh, because they threatened to disturb his monopoly on local power. He inflamed an already hot situation by importing three London constables and appointing 300 local special constables when he heard the inhabitants had guns and were drilling on the hills. He paraded his men on 29 April 1839 and the next day a meeting of angry Chartists took place at the Market Hall. The mob had a few weapons and Marsh, either in a calculated move to provoke a riot he could crush or in order to escape a crowd that frightened him, broke a window and shouted 'The people for ever!' If riot he sought, riot he got. One London bobby was beaten and badly hurt, the other two escaped, and the mob controlled Llanidloes until 4 May.

The occupation was peaceable – one man was ducked in the Severn for suspected stealing – but could not last. Troops arrived from Brecon to be met, as it was later said, by 'a rusty pistol . . . soapsuds . . . and women's tongues'. Thirty-two men were arrested, some of whom were sentenced to a savage fifteen years' transportation.

Although the Market Hall is the most photographed town building, there are others that should not be missed. The National Westminster Bank is housed in a superb half-timbered building (Elizabethan? No, 1926!) and Perllan-dy,

Orchard House, on the Llangurig road is an almost unique example of a mid-seventeenth-century merchant's dwelling. The church of St Idloes has already been mentioned, built as it is with bays from Abbey Cwmhir. Many consider it to be the finest church in Powys and it is certainly an interesting building with its modern 'school-room' extension tacked on to the ancient framework. If you walk twelve times around it on a special night, it is said you may look through the keyhole of the door to read the list of next year's dead. But which night is it that is so special?

There is also a Roman Catholic church, with a dedication to St Richard Gwyn, a local schoolmaster in the reign of Elizabeth I. He refused to take the oath of supremacy and to attend church and spent four years in jail; he was tortured and finally fined heavily. When asked how he would pay, he smiled and said, 'I have somewhat towards it – sixpence.' The joke went badly and he was sentenced to the full medieval execution: to be 'drawn on a hurdle to the place of execution where he shall hang half dead, and so be cut down alive, his members cast into the fire, his belly ripped unto the breast, his head cut off, his bowels, liver, lungs, heart thrown likewise into the fire . . .' and so on.

Gwyn asked, 'What is all this? Is it any more than one death?' In 1970 Gwyn was canonized, the only local Catholic saint. How would Gwyn have felt about a man who, half a century before Gwyn's appallingly blood end in 1584, sold 'pardons all hot from Rome' in the town market?

Beside its architecture and its place in the social history of Wales, Llanidloes is also rich in fairy lore. Near Llyn Ebyr, 5 kilometres north-west of the town, a shepherd and his wife had twin sons exchanged for fairy children. I have never understood why the fairies would want to do such things but that is by the by. The wife, alarmed by the sudden change of her children to ugly, grumpy babies, consulted the Llanidloes wise man. He suspected changelings and told her to prepare soup in eggshells for the local farm workers, and then to listen carefully. When the babies saw this they spoke quietly to each

other about the oddness of eggshells as soup bowls, thus giving themselves away, and were promptly thrown into the lake. The fairies rushed to their rescue and restored the original twins to their parents.

The town was famous for its conjurors and its *dynion hysbys* or cunning men. One once flew home to Cardiganshire from the town, taking with him a twelve-year-old boy who only realized why the journey had been so quick when he saw his garter at the top of a nearby ash tree. The conjurors offered cures for all complaints: to cure bed-wetting in children, give them gravy made from roast mouse; shingles could be cured by blood from a tom-cat's ear and warts by rubbing with the slime of a snail that was impaled on a thorn. As the snail shrivelled, so would the wart!

Our route leaves Llanidloes along Long Bridge Street. There are two bridges in the town: Short Bridge at the end of Short Bridge Street crosses the Severn before the Clywedog has joined it. The Long Bridge is beyond the confluence, an elegant structure and much less dangerous to the visitor. Lady Jeffreys, a local gentlewomen who died in the eighteenth century, became a water spirit and was 'prayed down' into a bottle and put in the river under Short Bridge. In 1848, when the new bridge was built, a boy found the bottle with its fly-like inhabitant buzzing angrily. Luckily his parents made him put the bottle back and it is still there to tempt the unwary.

Before you leave Llanidloes you should find a ladybird, for a local saying is associated with releasing the insect: 'Ladybird, tell me what the weather will be. If foul then fall to the ground; if fair, then fly in the air.'

The route now crosses Long Bridge and goes left on the B4518 for Clywedog and Machynlleth. At the second turning right, take the road to Van, an old village of terraced cottages beside ancient lead mines. The mines themselves are reached by going left at 949 875,

Van is the anglicized written version of the Welsh 'fan', the

The Severn at Llanidloes

Welsh 'f' being pronounced 'v'. Lead was found here by chance in 1862 and it quickly became apparent that it was one of the richest lodes in Wales – and at a relatively accessible point, only a couple of miles from the Severn valley. By the early 1870s the mine was producing quality ore in quantity, a £5 initial capital share being valued at £100. Sadly the prosperity was not to last, for by 1878 the world price of lead had fallen and by 1880 the richest lodes were all but worked out. Thereafter the story of Van was the sorry tale of all the Welsh metal mines – an unhappy list of new companies, bankruptcies and reduced output. In 1921 the mine closed for good.

The site is now a delight for the industrial archaeologist. There is an old railway (dating from 1871) to trace as it goes east to join the main line at Caersws, a row of terraced cottages and the site spoils itself. Our route passes the remains of the heavy brick walls of the ore washing trough, the piles of grey waste and Van Pool, said to have been formed by the waste-heaps rather than by nature. It is likely that the pool also served as a small reservoir for the site; today it is home to grebes and ducks.

Above us to the right, two chimneys emerging from the trees are pointers to the shaft site, though the shaft is thankfully blocked by waste. At that point there was also a water-wheel, mountain stream-fed, to pump the mines.

It is an interesting sidelight on modern attitudes that sites such as Van hold such a fascination. The ruins are evocative, the waste-heaps in no way incongruous; in fact they almost appear to enhance the surroundings by adding their touch of mystery. In Wales there are a number of sites like Van, the Cwmystwyth valley site being perhaps the loneliest and most atmospheric. In several places the sites have been opened as tourist attractions, most notably the Blaenau Ffestiniog slate mines and the Llywernog mine site on the Llangurig to Aberystwyth road. They are attractive for their glimpse of the past and the fascination with water-wheels, with buddles and

The ruins of the Van lead mine

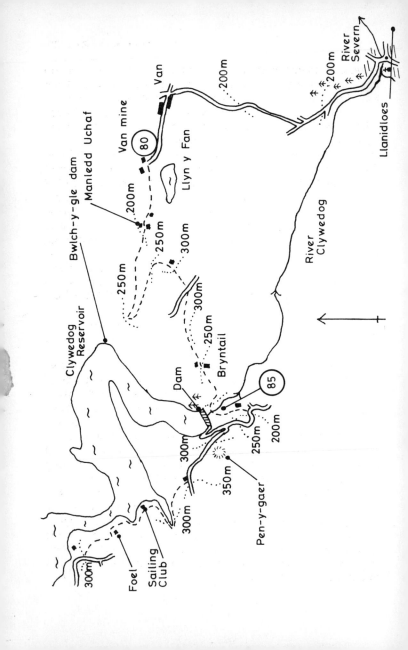

jiggers. If someone suggested a metal processing plant on Plynlimon today, we would be outraged. Will our defunct jam factories evoke Van-sympathies in our great-grandchildren?

Our route goes westward now, along the lane from the old brick piles to the house at the end. The County Council route here goes slightly south and then up the hill to Pen-y-clun, but this is not on a right of way and there is little indication that it is permissive. The right of way goes up the valley of the stream that feeds Van Pool, crossing the stream at 924 878 and contouring around the obvious encamped hillock to Pen-y-clun. Go up the farm lane to the road, across it and follow the path down to the old mines of Bryn-y-tail. Here, as if to prove the point, some buildings of the lead barytes processing plant have been restored.

After Van and Bryn-y-tail, sites redolent with decay, there is a culture shock ahead. The route from the barytes site emerges from trees directly underneath the 72-metre high white concrete Clywedog dam.

The dam is an impressive structure, irrespective of the merits or demerits of its position and the existence of the reservoir it holds back. The facts associated with such structures are awesome. It is 230 metres across at the top and its construction consumed a quarter of a million cubic yards of concrete. I doubt that it came in the conical, ready-mixed wagons we are used to seeing, but if it did there would have been a row of 40,000 of them waiting to discharge their loads. And there is a second dam, the Bwlch-y-gle, north-west of the point where our route crosses the B4518 and on that road. It is earth-made, the natural pass into the Van valley having been stopped up with 12,000 cubic yards of soil and debris. The Bwlch-y-gle dam is just a plug in the reservoir's bath – the main, or Clywedog, dam serving to regulate the flow in the Clywedog river and hence in the Severn. It is that purpose which explains the odd design. The slatted front of the spillway deflects water into the side channels and, in them, away from the dam's foundations. Without them the water might wear away the dam's base.

The scheme in the Clywedog valley was high-tech: the computer-aided design of the dam, the use of hydro-electric generators in the dam structure to power valves, calculations on volume capacity to ensure adequate flow in the Severn at all times but to allow the reservoir to catch flood waters – like a bucket under a leaking roof. But what of the Clywedog valley that lies drowned underneath?

No village lies below the surface to emerge at time of drought and haunt the designers, as happens at Vyrnwy and, more spectacularly, at Mardale-under-Haweswater in the Lake District. When the severe drought of 1984 hit mid-Wales the level dropped dramatically but all that was revealed was a brown tide-mark. What was swallowed here was good farm-land, a network of lanes and tracks and a way of life. The latter was under siege in any event, so let us not be sentimental because it is *de rigueur* to be so. Depopulation had carried on apace for many years, as the litter of derelict – and holiday – homes shows. The school in Staylittle closed not because the valley was flooded but because the valley had no children. Perhaps without the flooding (the reservoir was filled from 1966 to 1968) it would not have closed in 1975 – but it would have closed eventually.

The use of Welsh water to quench the Midland thirst is an emotive issue; the reservoirs of the Elan valley, as well as those on the Claerwen, Clywedog and Vyrnwy are obvious hooks for anyone wishing to hang out an ancient enmity to catch the wind. The Act of Union of 1536 did not at a stroke heal the wounds of centuries. The Clywedog reservoir is a beautiful sight from the viewpoint on the B4518 (a road that brought an old resident of Staylittle her first view of a motor car in 1968 – a mixed blessing), its nature trails are fine examples of their type, its water provides excellent sailing. However, I hope they drown no other mid-Wales valleys.

From the dam, Glyndwr's Way continues along the minor road that runs towards and along the southern edge of the

The view back to Van from the Way

reservoir. To the left at 908 869 is Pen-y-Gaer, the hill of the fort, the fort in question being an Iron Age hill-fort. The oval enclosure here is stone-walled, an unusual survival, though there are in fact a couple of others in old Montgomeryshire. At the south end the walls have been crossed at an angle to form a doorway at once defensible and difficult to attack. The massive width of the walls, some 4 metres thick, is impressive and, as is common in Wales, there is a local story that the site is druidic in origin.

Beyond Pen-y-Gaer, at the white house at 904 873, the route is signed right. Also signed here is the Clywedog Scenic Trail, and though that can be followed and, indeed, is worth the walk for its views, it goes off north-east following a spit of land to the water, while we go north-west also to water. The edge of the reservoir is followed to the road at 896 886. Go right and follow this road to Staylittle.

The road is not without interest and is very quiet. The Afon Biga is crossed – leading to the obvious inquiry about whether the 'Afon Smalla' will be crossed later – and a very fine crossroads is reached at 868 894. We turn right here, on to a road signed to Llanidloes. The left turn is also signed to Llanidloes and of course our road, the third of three at the cross, has come from Llanidloes!

When we crossed the Afon Biga we entered the Hafren forest. There are almost 50 square kilometres of it, with perhaps fifteen million trees. And yet in 1937 there were none. In very ancient times there may have been forest here – though of broad-leaved trees, not conifers – but when planting started, this was open moor. In its way the forest has had a more dramatic effect on the area than has the Clywedog reservoir which it dwarfs. The name Hafren is the Welsh name for the Severn. Hafren (or Habren) was the daughter of Locrinus, King of Britain, and his true love Estrildis. But Locrinus was married to Gwendolen, daughter of the King of Cornwall, and when he left her for Estrildis she raised an

The Clywedog Reservoir

army in Cornwall. The soldiers came here to fight Locrinus and he was killed. Gwendolen seized Estrildis and her daughter and threw them into the river to drown, realizing too late that it was all no fault of Hafren's and she should be honoured as her dead father's daughter. In remorse Gwendolen named the river for the girl. The Romans came and called the river Sabrina, their aspirant being 's' not 'h', and from that we have Severn.

Within the confines of the forest there is wild life, but the chief effect of all those trees is to have maintained the high Plynlimon wilderness by limiting access to it. As a result the moor is a wonderful place with a whole array of moorland birds to add to those that exist at the forest boundary and on the well-protected Hafren banks. Several times I have seen red kites above the Wye and Severn sources, indicative of a slow but thankfully steady expansion of their range. For those who are interested there are several very worthwhile walks in the forest and along the river, well waymarked and explained by leaflets, commencing from an information centre reached by turning left rather than right at the three-Llanidloes-roads crossroads.

There is information about the forest even on our route. As we follow the road through it, we can see that stands of trees have been planted, each with a nameplate to identify the species. The names are in English and Welsh; in Welsh the Japanese larch is *llarwydd siapon*, which makes it less alien somehow.

Beyond the forest, the route crosses the Afon Llwyd and comes upon a Glyndwr waymarker where none is needed. It could certainly be usefully transplanted from here to a point east of Llanidloes, or west of Welshpool.

Eventually the B4518 is reached again, a little way north of Staylittle, a tiny hamlet once buried in the remotest corner of the Clywedog valley. There are two stories to explain the odd name. One is that the position of the hamlet on a drove road

The Hafren Forest

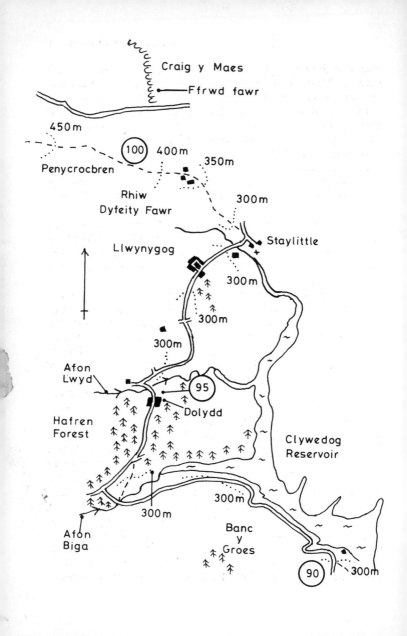

Craig y Maes

Ffrwd fawr

450m

(100) 400m

Penycrocbren

350m

Rhiw
Dyfeity Fawr

300m

Llwynygog

Staylittle

300m

300m

300m

Afon
Lwyd

(95)

Hafren
Forest

Dolydd

Clywedog
Reservoir

300m

Afon
Biga

300m

Banc
y
Groes

(90)

300m

and near the top of the Clywedog valley (the hamlet's Welsh name is Penfforddlas, the head of the green road) meant that travellers invariably stayed overnight. The other has the name derived from the expertise of the local blacksmith in the last century, who was so quick at shoeing horses that anyone on the valley road had only to stay-a-little!

Go left on the B4518 but only for a short distance. At the small Quaker cemetery, an unusual find in so remote a spot, turn left again at the signed lane that leads to Rhiw-defeitty-fawr farm (876 932) and on past the farm to reach open hillside.

The route actually heads uphill and west, towards the summit of Pen-y-Crocbren, but it would be missing one of the scenic highlights of the route not to go down to Dylife, and to continue east from there to Ffrwd Fawr and the head of the valley of the Afon Twymyn.

The head of the Twymyn valley forms a most impressive view: the steep slopes of scree with outcrops of hard sand-stone forming the crags of Creigiau Pennant to the west, the eastern slope being as steep but more pastoral. And so straight is the valley that it can be followed down to its confluence with the Iaen valley, all with a backdrop of the hills of Nant-yr-Eira. At this point we are only a matter of six miles from Llanbrynmair, also on our route. But do not be tempted to cut out the circuit westward.

The head of the Twymyn valley is geologically very recent, for until the last Ice Age the river flowed east, as it does to Ffrwd Fawr, before going south to join the Clywedog. When the ice came, the north-facing valley that stopped south of Pennant became choked, a small glacier formed and this cut the valley head back to intersect the Twymyn's course. The river was deflected northward and, more spectacularly, the hard sandstone horseshoe of Ffrwd Fawr was carved, drop-ping the river 45 metres to its new valley floor. Though not as high as the falls at Llanrhaedr-ym-Mochnant, Ffrwd Fawr is equally fascinating both for its volume of water – the river rises only 3 kilometres from the fall – and for the impressive

sweep of the rock amphitheatre over which the water hurls itself. Above the falls, the confluence of the streams that make the Twymyn is a beautiful spot with rowan, fern, rock and white water.

To the west of the falls is Dylife. It is difficult now to believe that this village once housed the thousand workers of a lead mine almost as rich as that at Van, and with a longer history of prosperity. It started before the Van mine, though its greatest period came in the third quarter of the nineteenth century when ore production reached 10,000 tons annually. There was high capital investment; a water-wheel 15 metres in diameter to drain the lower levels; houses, a church and inn. But there was always a transport problem, for ore had to be carried by pack-horse to Derwenlas, many miles to the west, and the mine could not survive a down-turn in lead prices.

A blacksmith at the mine, Sion-y-Gof – John the Smith – believed his wife had been unfaithful and murdered her. To provide himself with an alibi he also killed his daughter, throwing the bodies down a disused shaft and spreading the story that they had left him. Later the bodies were found and he was tried for murder, found guilty and sentenced to death. It was customary for the execution to be local and for the body to be gibbeted in an iron cage. As the village's only blacksmith, Sion had to make his own cage, his last work in his chosen profession. When it was completed he was hanged on Pen-y-Crocbren, the hill of the gallows. His body hung from the gallows in its gibbet cage until it rotted away. Then the gallows collapsed and the whole thing was buried in wind-blown soil. The hill name remained but the story became a legend. In 1938 two local men digging on the hill unearthed a cage; it had been fact, not fable, and the skull in its iron-piece is now in the St Fagan's Museum outside Cardiff.

The story adds to the chill of the wind that sweeps the hill, carrying down the spirit of Sion-y-Gof to join the ghost of a

The Twymyn Valley

village and the ghosts of the dead who lie beneath the shattered tombstones of the small cemetery.

Beyond Pen-y-Crocbren, which also has on its summit the remains of a small Roman fort as a military road came this way, our route emerges on to the mountain road through Dylife and follows it to 837 952 where a sign points left over the cattle grid. At 833 948 there are arrows pointing right (westward) along a distinct track towards the trig-pointed summit of Foel Fadian that was the highest point in old Montgomeryshire. Ahead of us here is Glaslyn, the blue lake, which legend states is bottomless. And beyond the lake is Plynlimon.

Our route does not go closer to Plynlimon than we are now, though technically we are on the flank of the hill mass that is covered by that name. But the range is so wrapped up with Owain that it would be a nonsense to ignore it. It was in these hills that Owain raised his standard, his two-legged golden dragon on a field of white. Today a plaque on a stone cairn at the eastern end of the Nant-y-moch dam commemorates that event. A couple of miles north-east is the Hyddgen valley, where Owain's initial small band fought the decisive battle that raised the pulse of the Welsh and spread the seed of revolution. At the site of the battle, two unhewn calcite blocks, the Glyndwr covenant stones, were placed.

I go often to Plynlimon to confirm again and again that I understand why Robert Gibbings wrote, 'Plynlimon is the kind of mountain I like . . . cliffs, but not formidable ones . . . buzzards soaring . . . ecstasy unbelievable'.

For me mountains are best described by a variation on the Chinese weather proverb: there are no bad mountains, only different types of good mountains. There are the scarp edges and secret lakes of the sandstone hills of the Brecon Beacons National Park, the wilderness of Elenydd, the breathtaking grandeur of Cwm Cau on Cadair Idris, the uncompromising terrain of the northern Rhinogs, the grassy whale-backs of the

Ffrwd Fawr

Carneddau. Plynlimon has a little of each, enough to keep the walker happy all day. And it has the sources of both Wye and Severn.

Plynlimon has a reputation – not entirely justified – for being boggy. One early explorer described it as a 'sodden weariness' – and Pennant would not come here at all: 'I was dissuaded from making it a visit, being informed that it was an uninteresting object, the base most extensive, the top boggy and the view over a dreary and almost uninhabited country'. Gilpin came, as the eighteenth century became the nineteenth, in search of 'the Picturesque', that strange system in which nature was marked out of ten against a set of laid-down guidelines for scenery. He was not impressed – 'there is not a sufficiency of water in the landscape to balance the land'. But then, Gilpin wanted to take a hammer to Tintern Abbey because it did not look right! In a famous passage, Peacock, the mid-nineteenth-century traveller, talked of anyone venturing out on the hill alone being 'little better than a fool' as he stood a 99 per cent chance of never being seen again. Peacock had become lost amidst thick black bog puddles that tugged at his legs, spirit and life. Today's walker – cocooned, if need be, against the elements in his rough-weather gear, and supported by the Ordnance Survey and quality compasses – can take a more relaxed attitude towards the hill. He is still there with the elements though and the wind blows as hard, if not as cold, even if you are nylon-clad. And it does seem that the wind is keener on Pen Pumlumon Fawr, where the *Mabinogion* described the Round Table Knights Kay and Bedevere sitting in the 'greatest wind in the world'. But that wind pays dividends if it wafts over your head a fork-tailed kite working the ridge for its breakfast.

From Glaslyn the track we are about to leave heads south-west, bridging Bugeilyn lake. From there open moor is crossed to join the Hengwm river that joins the Hyddgen where the battle was fought. The round trip is 16 kilometres, perhaps 21

Dylife

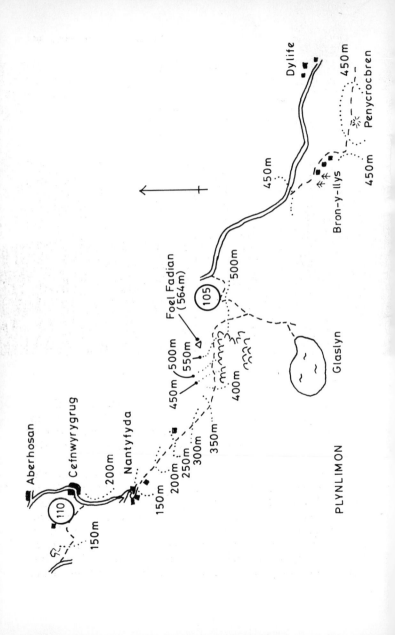

Plynlimon

if the summit of Pen Pumlumon Fawr is visited. Do it if you have the time. If not, come back to Plynlimon and to Hyddgen. Machynlleth is the place to find Owain the states-man and social reformer; Hyddgen the place to find the warrior.

Foel Fadian is, as I have said, the highest peak in old Montgomeryshire. The collecting together of the counties of 1536 Wales into larger units may have revived the ancient kingdom names, Gwynedd and Powys especially, and may have made government more efficient (though I am always reluctant to accept that changes brought about by bureaucrats for the sake of bureaucracy are ever in the interests of anything other than those concerned) but it has robbed Wales of the

undoubted individuality that its old counties possessed. I know that the district names are still the old county names but is that enough?

Our route does not climb Foel Fadian, though surely there would be few willing to pass up the opportunity, traversing along its southern flank above the tremendous gorge of the upper Afon Dulas. The view westward from this point is worth any effort to reach. It is so good – the rolling farmland of the coastal plain and the hills protecting it from Cardigan Bay – that it is difficult to leave.

The route does not follow the Afon Dulas, though that too has an appointment to keep in Machynlleth, but follows the Nant Fadian a little way north, to Nant-y-Fyda (810 961). From there take the lane to a road. The land and road are now following the Afon Dulas, the Nant Fadian having joined it at the farm. At 798 972 the Dulas is joined by another Afon Hengwm that has drained down northwards, from the watershed on Plynlimon.

By now the Dulas is large enough to carve a deep valley, wooded and very green. But we leave the valley beyond the telephone box, taking the signed lane left (south) at 797 972 towards the *isaf* and *uchaf* – the lower and upper – Cleirion farms.

At the first, the *isaf*, go right (westward) to climb Cefn Modfedd. This is a sudden and a little surprising piece of bare hill, but we soon exchange it for more farmland, descending the track to Blaen-y-pant (776 983). This lane swings sharply up left, giving fine views back towards Cefn Modfedd. Eventually, it makes a long sweep right through an unfenced field to a cattle grid at 777 984. Ahead now are superb views to Cadair Idris, a range that has increasingly dominated our view forward and, happily, will continue to do so for some kilometres though we lose the view for a time in the depth of the Dyfi valley.

At the cattle grid there is a no sign – by now we are used to

Foel Fadian

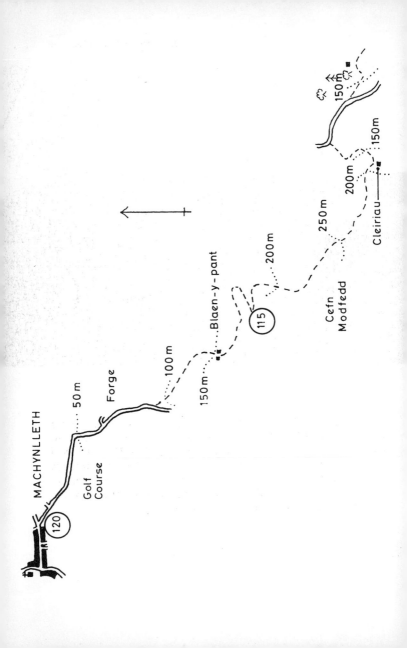

The Dulas Valley

this. Turn left along the hedge, turning north at the upper
Henllan farm (771 986) to go between the copses to a green
lane at 770 990, that is followed to the road at 765 994. Then
turn right to rejoin the Afon Dulas, which the road follows
into the delightful small village of Forge. Beyond the village
the unfenced road is followed over the modern battlefield, the
local golf course, and into Machynlleth.

MACHYNLLETH TO LAKE VYRNWY

As the town where Owain was crowned and where he held
the Parliament during which he laid down his ideas for the
social structure of an independent Wales, Machynlleth is the
focal point of our journey. It is also a lovely little market town,
set at the last point in the Dyfi valley where the river could be
easily negotiated before it flowed into its flood-plain estuary.
The town is well removed from the river, suggesting that the
Dyfi was never trusted.

The Romans came this way and had small forts, probably
little more than look-out points, on the hills of Wylfa and
Bryn-y-gog between which Machynlleth stands. The first of
these hills has an approach via 'Roman Steps' which seems to
prove the point, but they are almost certainly not Roman by
many centuries. One visitor to the town in the mid-nineteenth
century summed up this period in the town's history in most
eloquent style. 'The Romans fortified this place, to keep in
awe the mountaineers, who, many centuries after the Romans
had quitted our shores for ever, here established themselves
and bade defiance to their old enemies the English.'

The town's position on the Dyfi and mid-way between
Dolgellau and Aberystwyth has meant that it has always been
a centre for local trade. In 1291 Edward I granted a charter to
Owain de la Pole, lord of Powys, that he could hold 'a market
at Machynlleth every Wednesday for ever, and two fairs every
year'. It is too early yet to say if the market will indeed be
held for all of that time but it is still held now – the wide main
street, Maengwyn Street, is filled every week with the travel-
ling stallholders who make Welsh street markets so appealing.

The town is laid out along a formal T, though the right arm
of the T now straggles further than the left, towards the
railway which arrived in 1863. At the centre of the T is a clock
tower reminiscent of that in Knighton, erected in 1874 to
celebrate the coming of age of Viscount Castlereagh, eldest

son of the Londonderry family whose mansion was Plas Machynlleth. The Plas now houses the local government offices and is in need of a face-lift and a coat of paint. In front of it, though, the trees and rhododendron bushes of the old family's private garden are still a magnificent sight.

Elsewhere, the chief architectural interest in the town lies in its associations with the history of Wales. In Royal House – or at a house on that site – to the north of the Clock Tower, Davy Gam was imprisoned after his failed attempt to kill Glyndwr. It is not named from that event but from its use by Charles I in 1644 when the town lay on his route to Chester. And at the end of the lane beside Royal House is Gariswn Well, where the soldiers of the Earl of Richmond drank on 11 August 1485. The Earl stayed at Mathafarn, which we shall pass. His army was *en route* for Bosworth Field, where on 22 August the army of Richard III was defeated. The earl became Henry VII and so the Tudor dynasty began.

And on the northern side of Maengwyn Street is Owain's Parliament House. The present building, in dour stone and slate, is now believed to be later than the required date for Owain's Parliament, and it is by no means certain that it lies at precisely the right point. But tradition places the site here, and the building bows to this tradition with its 1404 Parliament House plaque and Owain exhibition. Beside it the Tudor-style building (but very recent – in fact 1911) houses the local Tourist Information Office. Further east, and on the southern side of the street, is another timber-framed building. This one is dated 1628 by inscription and, though it has been much renewed, is a rare example of such a style of building in this part of Wales.

For the rest, the town is Victorian. The church is interesting by virtue of being so English in appearance for a spot buried deep in Wales. Inside, it appears wide, having no colonnades, but the brightly painted wall and ceiling traceries do not seem right – even if they do hark back to pre-Puritan days when all churches were painted.

A figure on the Clock Tower, Machynlleth

One last treasure of the builder's art is the Dyfi bridge, about a kilometre north of the town. Since the reason for the town's existence is that the river could be crossed here for the last time, there has probably been a bridge over the Dyfi for many centuries, though the first record is for one built in 1533 for £6 13s 4d. The present bridge, an elegantly low, arched structure, dates from 1805 when its £250 construction cost was shared by the counties of Montgomeryshire and Merioneth-shire which were linked.

Although the Dyfi downstream of the bridge becomes increasingly wide and tidal, it is still surprising to discover that at Derwenlas about 3 road kilometres away (though twice that in river miles) from Machynlleth, there was a port. Derwenlas served Machynlleth's cloth industry as well as the slate quarries of Corris and the lead mines of Dylife. Machyn-lleth's wool was taken to Ireland, where it was exchanged for flax. If there was no return cargo, soil ballast would be taken on board and this would be dumped on the Dovey banks. The absence of snakes in Ireland led to the belief that Irish soil somehow repelled reptiles. Goodrich Castle in the lower Wye Valley had a floor of Irish soil to stop toads living in it, and here the local farms were advertised as snake-free if they had Irish soil dumped on their land. Strangely, they do actually appear to be snake-free!

Glyndwr's Way leaves Machynlleth eastward, along the A489. Cross the Afon Dulas and you come to Penegoes, a small village spread out for some way along the road. At the church, which is reached at the start of the village, an elegant slate tablet records that Richard Wilson, the famous landscape artist, was born here in 1713. It is an apt spot for the tablet since Wilson's father was rector of the church, though the St Cadfarch's that we now see replaced the medieval church as late as 1880.

The route continues through Penegoes and since the path out of it is unsigned, watch for a sign in English and Welsh

The Parliament House, Machynlleth

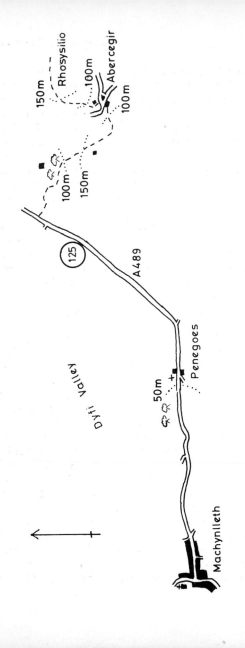

advertising cottage and caravans to let near houses at the top of a lane (788 025). A couple of hundred metres further north-east, the route takes the green lane right (south-east) through the set-back gate (789 026). To compensate for the road walking, this lane leads to some pleasant hill country and some spectacular views of Cadair Idris and the Dyfi valley. The Dyfi and Mawddach rivers are rightly famed for their scenery, but while part of the beauty of the Mawddach is at its estuary, where the broad river mouth is set off against the peaks on either side – the foothills of the Rhinogs and Cadair Idris – the Dyfi's estuary is less exciting, disappearing into a broad flood-plain. This provides interest of its own, as a trip to the RSPB sanctuary at Ynys-hir will quickly show, but it does not have the dramatic appeal of the Mawddach from Barmouth bridge. The Dyfi's charm lies in the section from here on, near Cemmaes Road, back to its birthplace – Craiglyn Dyfi beneath the Arans. The gentle curving hills, the long sweeping river, the greens and browns – it is delightful country.

The route follows the green lane and then a less wide but distinctive path around the flank of Bryn-wg, and down into Abercegir, which is entered past the ruin of a water-wheel powered flannel factory. Abercegir has a neatness that implies a real care for house and garden, and a calm that makes the heart ache to be part of the community that generates it. It is so quiet . . . So quiet, in fact, that at length you wonder whether all the cottages are holiday homes and whether the calm neatness is the peace and order of the graveyard.

For all that, the water stand-pipes in their brick niches are quaint and the seat that offers rest in front of one of the prettiest views in Wales must be appreciated. The route from the mill ends in Abercegir's main street. Go left and then sharply back right at the Y-junction, or go right and take the lane left to reach Bryngwawr bungalow (805 018), where a signed lane leads off up the hill. The track becomes less distinct but can still be distinguished as it reaches the ruin of Gader-goch (812 023). Once the summit ridge of Cefn Coch

has been reached the views are again to the Dyfi valley and Cadair Idris and remain so as a green lane is joined (825 029), and followed to a crossroad of lanes at 833 031. The latter stages of this route – with the deeply rutted lane in an avenue of wind-stunted oaks and the view northward – is quite beautiful. At the crossroads go left and down the lane to the main road at 825 044. Turn left here and up to the roundabout where the A470 for Dolgellau, going north-east, is taken.

Across the Dyfi from this point if Mathafarn. Though the house that now stands there is from the early seventeenth century, an earlier one on the same site has a place in history. It was owned by Dafydd Llwyd ap Llywelyn, a 'great poet and scholar' who was well known as an astrologer. When, in 1485, Henry, Earl of Richmond stayed the night on his way to Bosworth Field, he asked Dafydd if he was going to win the coming battle and Dafydd asked for the night to ponder. Dafydd was deeply troubled, presumably because there was no outcome to his ponderings, and his wife asked him why. When she heard the reason she was furious – not that her prophet-husband could not read the future, but that he was so lacking in common sense. Her solution was obvious – tell Henry he would win. If he did the Llwyd would find favour; if Henry did not win, he was hardly likely to survive long enough to come back and complain. Dafydd did as she suggested. Henry was delighted with the prediction, and 'borrowed' Dafydd's horse. After all, if the battle was to be won he would be able to return it!

Henry did win and Dafydd was rewarded, though whether or not the new king returned the horse, history does not reveal. The Welsh drew a moral from the story – '*Gynghor gwraig heb ei ofyn*' which, roughly translated, reads 'The unsought advice of your partner is worth taking'.

Glyndwr's Way crosses the Afon Twymyn, that has come from Ffrwd Fawr, and turns right (south-east) immediately on to a lane through a superb piece of oak-woodland and out on

Abercegir

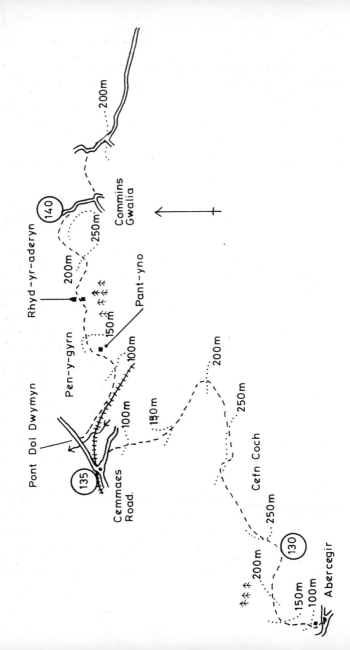

to a path between high ferns beside the railway line. Where the path divides (833 043) go left and up, heading, eventually, for a skyline TV aerial. The farm, Rhyd-yr-aderyn (843 047), is reached, and the lane from it followed to the lane at 854 048. Go right and down to the crossroads and there turn left. This lane becomes rough after the lane to Bryn-moel leaves it, to the right, but is easily followed, passing superb rowan trees, to the lane at 861 045. Turn right and follow this lane, bearing left at 862 043, to the main A470 at 878 036. This is a curious piece of land – unfenced, boggy moor, with patches of rosebay willow herb, that new weed – but then enclosed by sycamore, elderberry, ash and some conifer. At the lane end, go left to Llanbrynmair.

Here, in the seventeenth century, there lived a small colony of Flemish weavers who came to start a wool trade and succeeded despite having to pack-horse their wool over the high moorland to the north and on to Welshpool. The weavers were latecomers, for high on Newydd Fynyddog to the south of the village were two stone circles. They are beautifully sited, and such sites are so evocative; to be alone with them as the wind stirs the coarse hill grass is to feel the tug of the past. One circle is Lled Croen yr Ych, the width of the skin of the ox. Since such sites have always been tantalizingly mysterious, a local legend grew up that once in the valley there were two giant oxen who were eventually separated (but why?) on to hills on either side of the valley. There, alone but in view of each other, they bellowed in despair until they died. The larger one here on Newydd Fynyddog was skinned and its skin was pegged out to show later generations its true size.

Such folk stories are numerous in the Llanbrynmair district, which also abounds in odd cures and superstitions. Hereabouts if you came face to face with a frog or toad you had to close your mouth, because if it counted your teeth they would fall out. Warts were cured by leaving white pebbles in a parcel at a crossroads; the finder would open the parcel, take out the stones and transfer the warts to himself. And the locals cut their nails on a Monday so as to retain their complexions and figures. Here too they sang May carols, sometimes coupled with maypole dancing; these were sung outside houses, *canu don y pared* meaning sung under the wall, a custom so old – and probably pagan – that it had no folk memory or legend attached to it.

But most interesting of all was their name for the 'man in the moon' – *y dyn a'r baich draiu*, the man with the load of thorns, sentenced to exile on the moon for picking sticks on a Sunday – and *clwy'r edau wlan*, the 'woollen thread disease'. The local conjuror, effectively the witch-doctor, measured out a piece of yarn three times along the patient's arm from elbow to the tip of the middle finger. This yarn he wound around the patient's neck and then repeated a spell. The yarn was then remeasured twice; if it had shortened, the patient suffered from woollen thread disease, and could be cured by taking two draughts daily of a medicine of saffron with beer or gin, divided into seven equal portions.

Beyond Llanbrynmair our route crosses one of the loneliest stretches of moorland in Wales, though sadly it starts with a controversy. The Powys County Council route suggested that walkers used a stile, left, a couple of hundred metres along the A470 east of the village. No stile exists! A bridleway is marked from Coedcae Farm (904 026) but an inquiry in Autumn 1984 ruled that no bridleway exists! It remains to be seen whether a footpath is deemed to exist – certainly at the moment it is not easy to reach Cwm Carnedd (918 026) from Coedcae. Discretion, and ease of passage, suggest continuing along the A470 to 912 017, where a lane left by a telephone kiosk is signed to Hen Capel. This lane crosses the railway to reach the old chapel, a fine building where Samuel Roberts, the Utopian reformer, was once rector.

The lane beside the chapel is followed to Cwm Carnedd Isaf (917 026). The name, valley of stones, derives from a tumulus to the north near the spring of the Nant-yr-Eira, legendary

On the Way above Abercegir

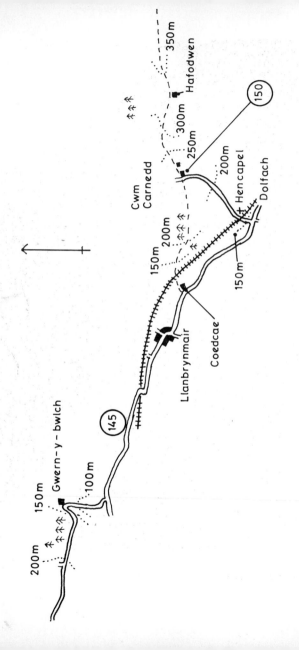

The Way near Commins Coch

burial place of a local robber called Owain who was caught when his stirrup broke as he tried to escape a group of local vigilantes, and was killed by them.

At Cwm Carnedd Isaf take the lane right (north-east) and go over to Hafodwen (928 027). From there a wet and indistinct track leads towards the forestry plantation which has been planted on the right of way. The only way now is to go north around the plantation, as the conifers are set so close that the forest is impenetrable to all but the most masochistic traveller. Beyond the northern tip it is worth going south along the forest edge to a fence going east at 938 030. Go east along the fence and watch for an old and faded blue arrow pointing diagonally left to a point on another fence, where the new Forestry plantation can be entered. This piece of moor is wet and miserable, and the next bit is little better. The new plantation pays no heed to the right of way and a route must be forged over draining ditches and through tiny trees to a lane past the ruins of Tyn-y-gors (944 028).

How would it have been to live at Tyn-y-gors, which despite its wind-break tree cover and the still-discernible remnants of a garden must have been a weather-swept and lonely spot? From the ruin the green lane runs up to the road at 947 029 and for the next few kilometres our route follows this road north-east.

There is something very special about following the Afon Gam through Nant-yr-Eira. The translation of the names gives us 'the crooked river through the vale of snow', which is poetic enough for a start. The river and the empty moorland stretching to the horizon emphasize the vastness of nature; it seems that the moor spreading evenly to the horizon must go on for ever. I can come here again and again, and still be thrilled by the barrenness.

At 964 066 we pass a lonely chapel. To come here, the locals must have believed hard in their God. Then at 975 074 a lane is taken to Dolwen farm and out on to the moor we have been

The railway crossing near Hen Capel

Hen Capel

watching from the road. Now for 3 kilometres that moor is real. Navigation is easy, however, taking a route below the hill-fort on Moelddolwen and then descending, using posts as guides, to a lane at 000 089. Perhaps I should be honest enough to suggest that on this last section of one of my favourite moors, it is worth having waterproof boots. The lane leads down to a road (008 100), at one point crossing a ford which is difficult to avoid. Go left, and down into Llangadfan.

The village takes its name from St Cadfan, one of the earliest Celtic saints, and there was once a local well named for him with healing waters. Cadfan was later the first Abbot at Bardsey island, where 20,000 saints were buried and to which three pilgrimages were the equal of one to Rome. In the yard of the church dedicated to the saint, there lies William

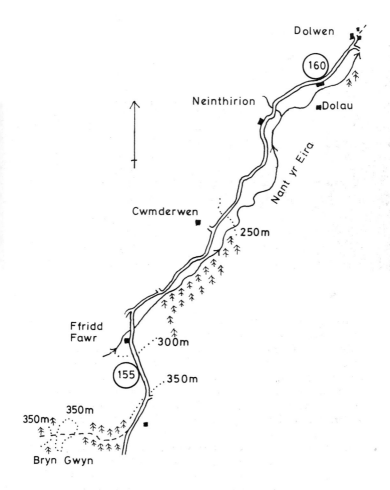

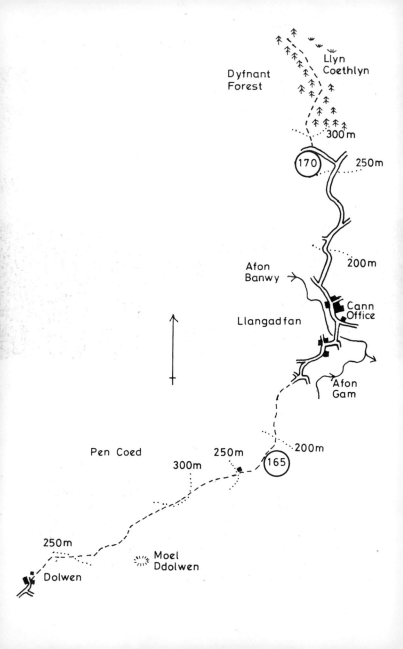

Nant-yr-Eira

Jones, an eighteenth-century 'scholar, philosopher and poet'. This is not a unique dedication, but Jones does appear to have been a fairly special character, a self-educated man who translated Roman poets into Welsh. In addition to his poetry he wrote articles on Welsh independence, which he fervently supported, and drew up some local pedigrees with a fine touch of xenophobia – 'I shall not take any notice of English pedigrees, lest I should trace their mushroom nobility to some bastards, arrant thieves, murderers, whether Saxon or Norman.' Jones was also a self-taught and self-styled doctor.

The Afon Gam, Nant-yr-Eira

He cured scrofula, and if asked to show a certificate showed instead the marks of the disease on himself!

Jones's grave can still be seen but to see one of the best houses of Llangadfan you must go to St Fagan's outside Cardiff, where Abernodwydd, a small thatched hall, has been re-erected.

At the main A458 road (012 107) the Cann Office Hotel is a famous old coaching inn; its curious name is an anglicized form of Cae'n y ffos, a fortified field. From the hotel go left along the A458 to 010 111 where the B4395 is taken north-wards. We are now looking for an unsigned but obvious road to the left at 010 126, just after a house to the right. Follow this to 009 128 where a signed path goes right (north) up the edge of a field and then between large clumps of forestry. This is the Dyfnant forest.

Within the forest the route is actually reasonably well signed with blue arrows and there is a good opportunity to view some of the 'other' conifers, for in addition to the Norwegian and Sitka Spruce there are Lodgepole Pines and Grand Firs. There are also a few, but excellent, broadleaves.

At 003 152 the route emerges on to a forest road. Go left, but do not waste too much time looking for the right turn at 002 154 as it is not there. Go on instead to Hendre Dyfnant (000 155), passing it and going right (east) at the road junction. Now follow this forest road to the road at Ddol Conway (014 174). On this final stretch there is some very fine scenery. Note especially the small rock outcrop or quarry on the left of the road, with its fine collection of shrubs and trees.

Go left at the road in Ddol Conway, then right on to an unsigned but obvious track that leaves the road at a shallow angle. A little way up this track our route joins the Craig Garth-Bwlch nature trail, jointly administered by the RSPB and Severn–Trent Water. At the approach to Bryn Conway (011 179) bear right and uphill. At 014 182, where paths go ahead and left, either way can be followed as they rejoin at 014 186. From there, follow the forest edge to the visitor's centre and Lake Vyrnwy at 016 191. At the centre, leaflets describing two Nature Trails are available. The first is the trail we have already covered part of; the second is the much shorter Grwn-oer trail. Both leaflets are worth obtaining; perhaps you will return to follow the trails or, if you are completing Glyndwr's Way from Welshpool to Knighton, you could use the Craig Garth-Blich trail to reach Ddol Conway.

Within the forest the bird life includes pied flycatchers, tree pipits, siskins and crossbills. The lake itself is home to the goosander – saw-billed ducks that nest in trees. Those who disbelieve this description may check its veracity in the RSPB's exhibition in the old chapel.

LAKE VYRNWY TO WELSHPOOL

In 1760 a Mr Probert proposed a scheme to drain the Llanwddyn Bog that lay around the village in the upper reaches of the Vyrnwy valley. He was convinced that the bog, about 5 kilometres long and 800 metres wide, could be turned into quality agricultural land. His scheme, which today would meet stiff opposition, never came to anything but a century later someone else was interested in the bog. However, Liverpool Corporation did not want to drain the bog; far from it, they wanted to use the water-bearing qualities to supply their thirsty city. In 1880 work on a dam began at the narrow eastern valley end, where a natural rock barrier was augmented by loose stone with a cement binder. The dam was no feat of modern engineering as at Clywedog. Here, though the roadway is elegant on its 33 arches and the spillway nicely faced, the dam is just a plug. Half a million tonnes of rock infill were used, with 27,000 tonnes of cement. The dam holds back a reservoir of over 60 thousand million litres of water, a lake with a surface area of about 450 hectares.

The reservoir brought fresh water to Liverpool, reducing deaths from cholera, but there was a cost. There were about 450 people living in the valley, mostly at Llanwddyn village about two miles up-valley of the present dam. To re-house them the Corporation took the remarkable action of re-siting the village, moving houses and even headstones and grave remains. The new village was sited beyond the dam and given the same name. It was an inspired answer to a human problem – and a by-product was that they moved the bodies closer to heaven, even if only by a metre or so.

When the Vyrnwy reservoir was constructed it was fashionable to plant the valley sides with conifers. There were several reasons for this. It was thought that the trees generated clouds and so enhanced rainfall and that they helped prevent contamination of the water supply. It is now considered that

The Dyfnant forest

neither of those ideas holds water as efficiently as the lake, but the trees are still there, lending an air of secrecy and intimacy to the reservoir. This air is further enhanced by the turreted water tower on the northern lake edge, a miniature of Castell Coch near Cardiff, which itself was inspired by the Rhineland castles. The tower, another remarkable piece of planning, is a straining tower where water is filtered before being passed to the three 106-centimetre aqueducts which carry the water on its 110-kilometre journey to Merseyside. This air of mystery makes it natural to add a local fairy story. A mischievous local goblin or spirit, Ysbryd Cynon, was eventually prayed down into a quill feather (!) and hidden under a stone at Llanwddyn. Sadly, this fact was forgotten and one day the lake-makers blew up the stone, Carreg yr Ysbryd. From the smoke and debris emerged a large frog, rubbing its eyes as if from a long sleep. It hopped away and has not troubled the valley since, although on some nights there is a noise as if someone, or something, is dragging chains.

The lake is encircled by a road that is rarely more than a stone's throw from the water, allowing every combination of sunlight and tree-shade to play their colouring tricks on the surface. In the long drought of 1984 the most westerly sections of the lake retreated and though old Llanwddyn was not revealed, there were old and bleached walls and tree-stumps near Pont Eunant, sticking up like fossilized bones from the hard, cracked mud.

Also near Pont Eunant is a road that crosses a few kilometres of barren moorland to Bwlch y Groes. Here, at the pass of the cross – legendary site of the rescue of a traveller from robbers by a ghostly Christian – there is a magnificent view of the Arans, a wall of mountains westward. From the pass a road drops steeply down south to the Mawddwy villages, home of the Red Brigands, an ancient mob of lawless bandits who were safe in their inaccessible valley and are

Lake Vyrnwy during a drought

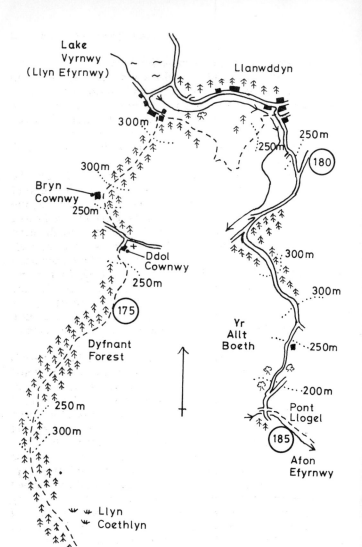

Lake Vyrnwy (Llyn Efyrnwy)

Llanwddyn

300m

250m

250m

180

300m

Bryn Cownwy

250m

300m

Ddol Cownwy

250m

300m

175

300m

Yr Allt Boeth

250m

Dyfnant Forest

200m

250m

Pont Llogel

300m

185

Afon Efyrnwy

Llyn Coethlyn

commemorated in the inn name at Mallwyd.

At the northern tip of the lake a road for Bala leads off north, crossing between high moorland on one side and the fine ridge of the Berwyns on the other. The Berwyns are worthy of the walker's interest, for although the area between Cyrnwy and Bala is moor rather than mountain, the ice-gorged cwms on the north-eastern face of the Berwyns break up the pattern.

Moorland Berwyn is a wild place. Here the Devil hunts the souls of the dead with the hounds of hell, a modification of an ancient Celtic legend that it was Arawn, King of the Underworld, who hunted, and that his snow-white, red-eared hounds could occasionally be heard. The noise might have been carried on the chilling east wind that sweeps the high plateau eloquently known as Gwynt Traed y Meirw, the wind from the feet of the dead. It blew in August 1165, driving cold rain into the face of Henry II so that after 'a few days he was oppressed by a mighty tempest of wind and exceeding great torrents of rain'. Henry withdrew and 'filled with a mighty rage he caused to be blinded hostages who had been held in fetters by him'.

North from Llanwddyn itself, a network of blind valleys is reached beyond the beautiful Cwm Hirnant and the Tanat Valley. At the head of the valley beyond Llanrhaeadr-ym-Mochnant is Pistyll Rhaeadr, the highest waterfall in Wales; it falls, at half height, behind a natural arch and has long been considered one of the Seven Wonders of Wales. At the head of another valley is the old church of Pennant Melangell, named from an Irish virgin saint. In AD 604 the saint, also known as Monacella, was confronted by Brochfael Ysgithrog, Brochfael the Fanged, as he hunted hares near where she had lived as a solitary for fourteen years. Melangell was praying and the hare hid beneath her skirts, the dogs standing off spellbound. Brochfael gave her land for a nunnery. The church at the valley head is architecturally of enormous interest, containing sections of a twelfth-century shrine to the saint.

Our route leaves Llanwddyn on the B4393 for Llanfyllin,

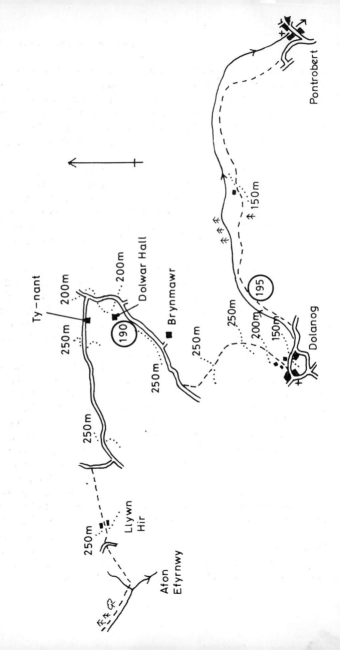

passing the turning for Cwm Hirnant. At a left bend that is almost Alpine in its sharpness and steepness (035 183), go right on a minor road heading south. This road is followed to 029 176 where a lane goes off left and up into the forest. The lane is followed all the way to Llywdiarth (032 156); there are occasional blue arrows along it but it is always obvious as the major forest road.

At Llywdiarth go right (south) on the B4395 passing a finely sited church and reaching Pont Llogel on the Vyrnwy river. To the right here is Llywsdiarth Park, once home of the influential Welsh family of Vaughn. Sir Gruffydd Vaughn was one of Glyndwr's allies in the rebellion. The route actually goes left (east) just before the bridge, following the river into the forest.

At 041 149 the Nant Llywdiarth joins the Vyrnwy but we leave it to go north-east and up, crossing farm land to the minor road at 045 152. Cross the road and walk on up the farm track to Pentre-herin (056 153) and another minor road. Go right here, following the road to 056 151 where there is a long right-hand bend. Here a track goes off to the left. Follow this to the B4382 at 075 153, then go right (south).

The road passes Dolwas Hall, a long cruck-framed house, and reaches the lane to the white-porticoed Dolwar Fach. Now rebuilt, this was once the home of Ann Griffiths, the late eighteenth-century hymn writer. Just beyond the lane to Dolwar Fach, at 065 142, a signed footpath leaves the road to the left (south). The footpath climbs the hill of Allt Dolanog but does not reach the hill-fort known as Llys y Cawr – Giant's Court – on the summit, as it contours around the eastern slopes to reach a lane (069 132). Follow the lane to Dolanog.

A sprawling village, Dolanog is nevertheless beautifully set on the Vyrnwy. In the lower part of the village an old bridge, with even older safety rails, crosses the water from a huddle of houses. Further upstream the river tumbles over a waterfall that is in part man-made, in a cascade that is very picturesque. The weir once drove a water-wheel for a grain and fulling mill that still stands, though it is now a private house.

From Dolanog, Glyndwr's Way follows the Vyrnwy. Go left over a stile from the B4382, east of the old bridge. Follow the path as it crosses a stream running into the Vyrnwy and then hugs the river bank, swinging around the base of Pen y Berth. The hill was once famous for its springs which were believed to cure eye disorders.

The path along the Vyrnwy is a delight, the river well set off by the wooded northern bank. We leave the river, however, to reach Gwern-fawr (088 134), then to follow a lane that runs past Doladron farm (102 134) and on to a minor road (103 128). Go left and on into the hamlet of Pontrobert.

The name of the hamlet derives from the name for the Vyrnwy bridge, itself named after Oliver ap Robert who, in 1670, was the first to bridge the river at this point. Do not miss the cruck-framed cottage. Go over Oliver's bridge and turn right, then go left after the chapels. At 112 127 there is another chapel, opposite which is a 'No through road'. Go along this and the track from Bryn-y-fedwen (116 126). This latter track passes north of Dolobran Hall, home of the local family of Lloyds whose small banking business has grown into a household name. The Lloyds were Quakers and east of the hall is a Quaker meeting hall in which, it is thought, William Penn preached before leaving for America and the founding of Pennsylvania.

South-east of Dolobran Hall, and on the other side of the Vyrnwy, is Mathrafal which is strongly believed to have been the site of the court of the princes of Powys, who moved here to escape the border incursions of the Mercian Saxons when their court was at Shrewsbury. The site was used until the twelfth century, when Gwenwynwyn moved his court to the stronger Powis Castle. After the prince had departed, it remained a fortress, finally being totally destroyed by King John in his campaign against Llywelyn the Great.

Our route joins a lane at 130 125 that leads to a minor road at 139 125. Go right here, and take the signed path left at 141

Dolanog

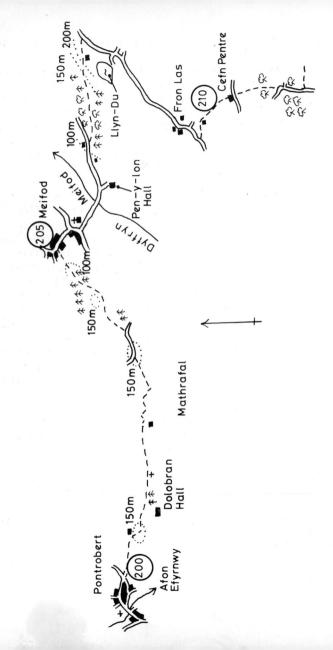

126 that leads through trees to Gallt yr Ancr, the rock of the anchorite, named from St Gwyddfach who was a hermit living in the outcrops on the hill in the early sixth century. There are several trenches cut around the hill, suggesting an ancient fortress, but one is more recent, having been cut by locals convinced that a chief was buried here and that his grave contained treasure. Beyond the hill the pathway descends eastward through trees to the road at 151 135. Go right here and into Meifod.

The Vale of Meifod, Dyffryn Meifod, is formed between the Broniarth Hills to the south-east and Allt Main and Gallt yr Ancr to the north-west. Though it is, in fact, just a part of the valley of the Afon Vyrnwy, it has a distinct identity separate from that of the valley running down from Lake Vyrnwy itself. A mile or so upstream the river has turned sharply northward, giving the Vale its southern end, and in the Vale it runs in a wide flat plain; there is even an ox-bow lake, almost perfectly horseshoe-shaped – a geography teacher's dream! For a long time the special nature of the Vale has been noted. Cynddelw, a late twelfth-century bard, loved the grandeur of Gwynedd, 'the spot whose surface is trodden by the brave'. But the Vale was 'A privileged sanctuary, a bright cultivated spot – Fair Meifod.' Six centuries later Sion Yshgrifen referred to 'Meifod's Vale most fair'.

The name is not well understood; it could just mean summer pasture but is almost certainly pre-Christian, for Meifod was an important site in the Celtic Christian church and would have adopted a *llan* name if it had not had a name already. The site was chosen by St Gwyddfach and the first church that was built here was dedicated to him. A second was built later, dedicated to the better known St Tysilio, a son of Brochfael the Fanged, prince of Powys. At that time Meifod was the foremost church of Powys and the princes were buried in it. Within the present church, St Mary's, is an old inscribed stone believed by some to be monument to a later prince, Madoc ap Maredudd. If it *is* Madoc, who died around 1160, then it dates from the time of the first construction of

The inscribed stone, Meifod church

the present church. Some experts, however, believe that the stone is much older, perhaps as early as the ninth century, pointing to the Vikingesque style of some of the carvings in support of this theory.

The churchyard covers nine acres, encompassing the sites of the two earlier churches and a great deal more besides. With the wide street outside and the far-flung houses, it gives Meifod a roominess unlike other Welsh villages. The dominance of the huge church site is an indication of the importance that spirituality has always played in Meifod's history. Today there are four chapels or churches, which is more than the number of inns by a goodly factor.

We leave Meifod between two chapels, going east and crossing the Vyrnwy, which we have crossed several times before, for the last time. At the road fork (159 128) go left and take the signed footpath at 164 129 that goes east and up through the forest. Where it emerges from the trees the path is above Llyn Du, the Black Lake, a small stretch of water but a magic stretch, reputedly unfathomable.

Further east, at 177 130, the path reaches a road. Go right (south) along it, then over at the crossroads and on to a road fork at 166 117. To the right here, below the afforested hillfort, is Cobham's Garden where in 1417 Sir John Oldcastle, Lord Cobham, was captured. Cobham was a Hereford man who served Henry IV and Henry V loyally and bravely in battle, but unfortunately he was a Lollard, a follower of Wycliffe and his outlawed religious sect. As a result Cobham was imprisoned in the Tower, but escaped in 1413 and came here to the Meifod area, where he sheltered with Lollard friends in the woods. Many knew where they hid but no one would say until someone betrayed them for the thousand mark reward that Henry V was offering for their capture. Cobham was taken at his 'Garden', though he put up strong resistance in which his leg was broken. He might have escaped but for this; apparently the leg was broken by a local woman, using a stool. Cobham was taken to London where he was tried and condemned. He was dragged on a hurdle to

St Giles's Field and hanged from a gallows by a chain around his waist over a slow fire which consumed both him and the gallows.

At 166 117 turn right and watch for the hidden green lane to the left at 164 116. It looks an unlikely path at first but there is an old and decaying blue arrow beside a stile. The path then improves, passing Cefn Pendre farm (168 112) and emerging on to a road at 170 105. A dyke to the left here is said to be part of the outer defences of Mathrafal Court. Go left at the road (southwards) and downhill to 169 103 where an unelaborate gate to the left allows access to a field. Go down to, and over, the stream and on to the caravan park ahead, at Pant (175 103). From the park take the lane to the B4392 at 177 101, then go left along the road.

At 194 106 turn right and follow the road to the crossroads at 210 085. Here go across and follow the track to Welshpool.

Welshpool is another 'gateway to Wales', though one that because of its position on the Severn is more deserving of the name than most. In appearance it is a Georgian market town, more English than Welsh since we can, after our long trip through the Welsh heart-land, recognize Welsh character-istics. In my assessment of the town as 'English' I am at odds with Leland who in the reign of Henry VIII found the town 'wel buildid after the Walsch fashion', but would find favour with Defoe who found it a 'good fashionable place and has many English dwelling in it and some very good families'. This is unusual for I rarely agree with Defoe!

The town is probably named from the de la Pole family, descendants of Gwenwynwyn, and was at first known as Pool, the 'Welsh' being added to avoid confusion with Poole in Dorset. In Welsh it is Y Trallwng, which could signify boggy, but is more likely connected to the legend that one day the town will be swallowed by the waters of Llyn Du, another Black Lake, this time in the parkland of Powis Castle.

In the centre of the town there is a house with an inscription that tells us that an ancestor of the builders, one Roger Jones, was in the reign of Edward IV the first Jones in Wales. He has

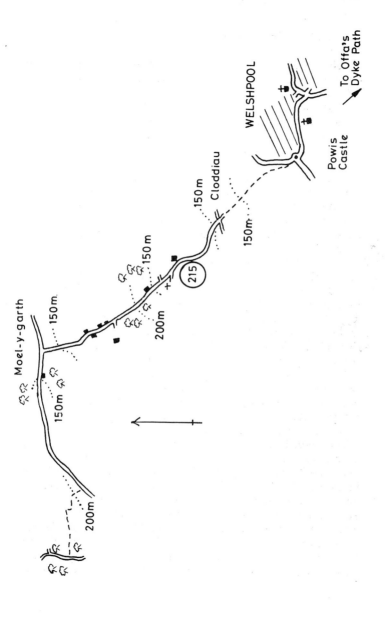

t*ough* to answer for, *as* any glance in a Welsh telephone directory will prove. Since *Welsh*pool is our terminal town it is best to *disco*ver it at leisure – *it* will reward your interest. But do not miss *the* Shropshire Union Canal, and one of the Great Little Trains of *Wales*, that arrives *here* from Llanfair Caereinion.

But most of all do not miss *Pow*is Castle, home *to* the princes of Powys. Originally there *was* a motte and bailey castle here; the present castle – built of *red* sandstone and known not unnaturally as Castell Coch, the Red Castle – was constructed near this site by Gruffydd ap Gwenwynwyn. Unfortunately, Gruffydd was involved in a plot to overthrow Llywelyn the Great and for his pains his castle was destroyed. The present building dates from about 1275, though there have been many additions and alterations since then. When the male line from Gwenwynwyn died out Hawise, the sister and heir of the last of the line, married John Charleton, a Shropshire man. Charleton lent his bloodhounds to help the search for Cobham, the Hereford Lollard, and was cursed to be unhappy. A gifted hermit was brought to lift the curse but he could not and Charleton died a miserable man. After his death the castle was owned by more Charletons, then by the Greys and the Herberts. William Herbert held the castle for the Royal cause in the Civil War but it was taken by the forces of Sir Thomas Myddleton, though Cromwell intervened to stop its demolition by the occupying Roundheads. The castle was restored to the Herberts and passed by the female line to the Clive family, famous for their exploits in India. The family are the current holders of the Earldom of Powys and occupiers of the house – it has been continuously occupied for 700 years – though it was given to the Treasury in 1952 in lieu of death duties. It is now administered by the National Trust and is open to the public in the summer months, when the visitor can enjoy not only the architectural beauties and luxurious decorations of the castle itself, but the superb gardens laid out

The Shropshire Union Canal, Welshpool

in formal style on seventeenth-century terraces. The terracing did not meet with the approval of Capability Brown, who landscaped the park. He wanted them 'ruggedized' into crags. And Pennant thought they were in 'imitation of the wretched taste of St Germain en Laye'. I prefer the natural to the formal, but I do like the huge yew hedges. On one trip I saw an immense ladder laid up one yew so that it could be trimmed. The man with the shears was earning his money.

THE RETURN JOURNEY: OFFA'S DYKE

At Welshpool, Glyndwr's Way can be linked to the Offa's Dyke long-distance footpath which, since that route also passes through Knighton, allows a continuous route to be made through mid-Wales, virtually from border to sea and back.

To join Offa's Dyke from Welshpool, cross the Shropshire Union Canal on the B4381 and follow that road to Lower Leighton (244 066). Go left and follow this road to 248 076. Here turn right up Hope Lane through the village of Hope, to join Offa's Dyke at 257 073.

To join Offa's Dyke from Powis Castle go south on the A483, and then the A490 through Cilcewydd to the junction of this road with the B4388 at 238 020. The B4388 southward from here is the Offa's Dyke Path.

From Hope, Knighton is about 45 kilometres; from the junction of the A490 and B4388 it is about 35 kilometres. Between the two, the Offa's Dyke Path passes through some very fine countryside, as well as the town of Montgomery.

Powis Castle

Owain Glyndwr's Rebellion

> . . . At my birth
> The front of heaven was fully of fiery shapes;
> The goats ran from the mountains, and the herds
> Were Strangely clamorous to the frighted fields.
> These signs have marked me extraordinary,
> And all the courses of my life do show,
> I am not in the roll of common men.

Though these are the words of Shakespeare (from *Henry IV*, Part One), they are based on the Welsh legends surrounding the birth of Owain Glyndwr. It was also said that on the night of his birth his father's horses were found in their stable, standing in blood up to their fetlocks. And that when Owain was still a baby in arms the sight of a sword or spear would start him shrieking, a shrieking which could only be silenced by his touching the weapon.

Such legends often grow up around the birth of famous men and in Owain's case very little is actually known of his early life – to such an extent that not even the date of his birth is established with any accuracy. He first enters history as a witness in a long drawn-out case in the Chester courts: the case of Scrope *v* Grosvenor which concerned the right to a particular coat of arms. Since it lasted for nearly five years it must have been of tremendous importance to the contestants, an importance not readily understood in our age when heraldry, if it is considered at all, is viewed in the kindly light used to illuminate British eccentricity. In the late fourteenth century such was not the case, however, for the right to arms

The memorial to Llywelyn the Last, Cilmery

was vital to any gentleman. On 3 September 1386 one who gave evidence was '*Oweyn Sire de Glendore de age XXVII ans et pluis*'. One immediately obvious fact is that the entry in the court record is in French, still the language of the nobility. What we glean from the entry, apart from the difficulty which the clerk to the court experienced in producing a respectable representation of Welsh names, is that in 1386 Owain was twenty-seven '*et pluis*'. The additional French phrase is awkward for anyone trying to pinpoint his date of birth. Its meaning is not dissimilar to 'over twenty-one', but it can also mean 'at least' since in those days age was not treated with the mixture of reverence and fear that we employ today. At the same trial Geoffrey Chaucer gave evidence, and he is listed as being 'forty *et pluis*', when good historical evidence suggests he was forty-six at the very least. It is difficult to believe that Owain just wanted to be 'over twenty-seven'. We can conclude that he was born probably in 1359, perhaps a few years earlier. From other evidence the dates 1349 and 1354 have been suggested; however, the earlier date seems to make him too old at the start of the rebellion and far too old at the finish, while the later date is to an extent discredited by the same source suggesting that Owain died when he was forty-six. Since it is thought he was alive in 1415, there is thus a contradiction.

Remarkably, in view of the position Owain now holds in the hierarchy of Welsh heroes, not only is the date of his birth unknown but also the place of his birth, for all the blood on his father's horses' fetlocks! It is widely assumed that he was born at one of the family's two Powys estates, but some stories have him born near St David's, in old Pembrokeshire, in the house of his aunt. Later in life, when Owain was looking for support from the whole of Wales for his claim to the princehood, his mother's descent from the royal house of Deheubarth was invaluable. The Pembrokeshire connection might have evolved then.

Owain's father, Gruffydd Fychan, died when Owain was still a boy. Gruffydd Fychan – Griffith the Younger, son of another Griffith – was descended from the royal house of Powys. He could also trace a line back to Rhodri Mawr, and since Rhodri was at the head of royal houses of Gwynedd, Powys and Deheubarth, Owain's lineage was a fine one. However, it was to the Powys house that they were closest and their holdings lay in 'Powys the bounteous and benign', as the greatest Welsh poet Dafydd ap Gwilym expressed it. Dafydd died in Owain's youth but the beauty and energy of his poetry, his love of nature and his humour touched the bards who later sang the praises of Owain's family, estate and princehood.

In the Welsh of the day Owain was Owain ap Gruffydd, heir to the family estates at Glyndyfrdwy and Cynllaith. The former is a name now taken by a hamlet beside the A5 road mid-way between Llangollen and Corwen, though the earlier name would have applied to a wider area. By a quirk of county boundary, Glyndyfrdwy now lies in Clywd. The name means 'the Gorge of the Waters of Dee'. The Dee (in Welsh the Afon Dyfrdwy) is a beautiful river. Rising from the north-west tip of Llyn Tegid – Bala Lake – it cuts a channel between the high moorland of the Berwyns to the south and that of Migneint to the north. Its valley is also well defined, but at Corwen after it has flowed north-east, it turns sharply eastward towards Llangollen and England. From here, at first it flows in a deep valley, a gorge defended at one end by Caer Drewyn and at the other by Castell Dinas Bran. This gorge formed the basis of Owain's local estates and gave him his name which, though variously rendered down through the ages, is now accepted as Glyndwr. Within the valley Owain had a lodge, the remains of which – only a tree-topped conical mound – are still visible beside the A5 at 125 431, just under 3 kilometres west of Glyndyfrdwy hamlet. Today the shouts which usually fill the valley are from the canoeists who face the white waters of the Dee near Llangollen, though it is a sad irony that Owain's ghost, if it sat among the trees at the side of the old lodge, would have a very fine view of English invaders speeding along the A5 into the heart of Gwynedd.

The second of Owain's estates, Cynllaith, lay on the other side of Berwyns from Glyndyfrdwy, where the Cynllaith brook runs into the Tanat. Here, at Sycharth, Owain had his chief house, for although his name derived from the estate on the Dee, the farmland was better here. Perhaps too, in this lusher and more sheltered valley, life was easier and more relaxed.

Information on Owain's early life is scant and has to be inferred from snippets in chronicles of the time, from the songs of the bards and from knowledge of the general lifestyle of the sons of the nobility of that time. One chronicler tells us that Owain was sent 'to be an apprentice of the law at Westminster' – that is, sent to the Inns of Court in London, though this is not absolutely certain as no records exist for the Inns at that time. The immediate implication of this is that Owain was being raised in the manner of the *English* nobility and such is indeed the case. The Inns were not just the centre for anyone wishing to be trained as a lawyer, but acted as a public school for the sons of rich families, giving a good general education in the ways of government and of society.

Owain would have spent many years at the Inns of Court, perhaps as many as seven, and on leaving would have continued his education in the ways of the ruling elite by becoming a squire in one of the better houses of England, to tend to his lord particularly in battle and in tournaments as well as to learn how to be a soldier. Owain was squire to Richard Fitzalan, the Earl of Arundel, who appears to have taken the young heir under his wing when his father died. Almost certainly he was also squire to Henry Bolingbroke – King Richard's cousin and, later, Henry IV. If this was indeed true, it was ironic that the close association of lord and squire should produce enemies at a later time. By then of course, the two had grown both up and apart. There may have been some personal animosity and Owain may have supported Richard as many Welshmen did – a policy unlikely to have endeared him to Bolingbroke.

We know something of the training that Owain would have

received as a squire, for although no personal record of his service exists there are contemporary accounts of the life of others. He would have run long distances and performed exercises in armour, to toughen him up, and would have practised long and hard with sword, mace and lance. But just as we know little of any other part of his younger days, we cannot positively identify any campaign in which Owain took part. The Welsh bards – chiefly Iolo Goch – picture him in Richard's Scottish campaign of 1385. There, so they say, he cut a fine figure with his shining helmet sporting a scarlet flamingo feather; his lance shattered but he used the jagged end to drive on the Scots before him 'howling with fear like wild goats' in an attack so savage 'that no grass nor corn would grow in his tracks'. The same bards describe Owain at a tournament 'resplendent in gold and scarlet trappings of the finest kind' and 'shattering their bodies and overthrowing a hundred knights'. It seems likely that in true Celtic fashion the bards overstated their case both for dramatic effect and to create the heroic leader that the native stock required. Certainly Richard did not honour Owain for his services in the Scottish campaign.

The last comment must not be seen to imply that Owain may not have had a distinguished military career. Detailed studies of his likely active service, in continental Europe as well as Scotland, suggest he may have been a seasoned campaigner, and while probably guilty of embellishing the truth the bards were almost certainly not liars.

By 1398 Owain's military career was seemingly over. He was now about forty, perhaps forty-five, and had settled down to a quiet life at Sycharth.

As a young man Owain had married Margaret Hanmer, daughter of Sir David Hanmer, a judge of King Richard's Bench and head of a rich and influential Flint-based family of Anglo-Welsh gentry. The bards who praised Owain loved her too: she was 'the best of wives' and 'of a knightly family, honourable, beneficient, noble'. The children of the marriage did not escape the same fulsome praise – they were 'a beautiful nest of chieftains'. Although the evidence of the number and names of Glyndwr's children is scant and some-times contradictory, what is sure is that the Glyndwrs had a large family. Of sons Gruffydd, Maredudd and Madog seem definite, but Thomas, John and David are also named. Of daughters there were many: Isabel, Elizabeth, Janet, Margaret, Catherine, Jane and Alice are named, though it may well be that Alice and Elizabeth are the same girl, or possible that Alice and Catherine were one and the same! Most sources suggest nine children, which certainly implies that Owain's wife Margaret was a strong, healthy woman. In late four-teenth-century Britain, childbearing was a risky business.

The same bards who described Owain and his family, albeit with perhaps more enthusiasm than accuracy, also described Sycharth. It was a wooden house, at first considered a strange construction at a time when the still-Norman English were living in huge stone castles. Owain's position was different however, for though he was a noble with contacts in English aristocracy, he was still a Welshman – a man from a subser-vient race. Barely a century had elapsed since King Edward's ring-of-stone had been tightened around the Welsh throat, and no Welsh noble was yet in a position to build in anything but timber, an inferior material.

Sycharth was protected by moats, and had nine rooms for guests with linen as fine as any in London's Cheapside. Outside were fishponds and a dovecote, peacocks and a herd of fallow deer. The entertainment was luxurious and no one was turned away. Today all that remains of this most splendid of halls is a grassy bank, with the remnants of the moat still visible, standing beside a minor road that follows the Cynllaith stream southward from Llansilin, a hamlet 10 kilometres west of Oswestry.

To maintain his house, with its minstrels and bards and 'ale from Shrewsbury town', Owain had an income of around £200 per year which was more than adequate for the task. The income was derived from his estates and so it was doubly important to him when, in 1399, his neighbour Reginald Grey,

Lord of Ruthin, stole some land on the Glyndyfrdwy estate. Owain was legally trained; he was a cultured man speaking Latin and French as well as English and Welsh. Despite his military background he chose to fight Grey in the courts, not on the battlefield. In the ordinary course of events he would have been successful – but times were not ordinary.

Richard II was a man of taste, but of expensive taste. Before he was old enough to hold the reins of power for himself, England had been governed by barons led by John of Gaunt, head of the house of Lancaster. Once Richard became old enough he offended these barons frequently, raised the exchequer levy on them and silenced their opposition by murder or exile. One to be exiled was his cousin Henry Bolingbroke, son of John of Gaunt. By 1399 Richard was all-powerful but naive enough to assume he could remain so despite his actions. He sailed for Ireland, to glory in the conquest of new lands and to extort more taxes. But as his ship pulled away from England that of Henry Bolingbroke was heading towards it. Richard rushed back from Ireland, landing at Milford Haven and making for Conwy. Significantly, he had chosen Wales as his base. At Conwy he was met by Henry Percy, Earl of Northumberland, who persuaded him that Bolingbroke meant him no harm but wished only to re-inherit his father's land and title. Richard rode to meet Henry at Flint Castle but was ambushed and captured. He 'willingly' abdicated in favour of Henry, retired to Pontefract Castle in Yorkshire and was never seen again.

At Conwy the royal baggage train was captured by Henry's followers but the Welsh, recognizing the treason of Henry's actions, 'liberated' the baggage and its wealth of silver and gems. Later most of the baggage was recovered, but Henry was not interested in 'later'; he wanted it now. Richard had been pro-Welsh and the Welsh liked him, for all his faults – though it has to be admitted his pre-Ireland tax rises had been unpopular and they had not rushed to join him as he travelled from Milford Haven to Conwy. The Welsh also had the royal baggage, and for both these reasons Henry IV was not well disposed towards them.

Following Glyndwr's rebellion, there was a persistent story in Wales that at one time he had been a squire to King Richard. It has even been suggested that he may have gone to Ireland with the king and been at Conwy when he met Northumberland. The latter could be true even if Owain had not gone to Ireland, for it would have been no great effort to travel from Sycharth to Conwy and if he was there he would have been seen by Northumberland. Owain was a fine figure of a man, very tall and wearing his hair long, down to his shoulders, at a time when the norm was hair close-cropped to suit wearing a helmet.

In the circumstances Owain stood little chance with his lawsuit in the English Parliament; the barons of the new King had as little time for the Welsh as had Henry himself. The Bishop of St Asaph exhorted the king and Parliament to be wary of creating new enemies before the ripples of the change of order had died away, but to no avail. Owain's case was not only dismissed – bad enough in itself – but with the comment: 'What care we for barefoot Welsh dogs.' For a proud man of royal blood it was a humiliating experience. And one not to be forgotten.

1400

In Wales, all was not well. Richard's army disbanded into Wales, some of the soldiers sickened by the way Bolingbroke had deceived their king and usurped his throne. Others were just at odds with the world, in the way that old campaigners can be. Talk that Richard had been murdered made the angry seethe even more, and rumours that he was alive and a prisoner made them long for justice. When Henry IV raised the taxes, the temperature of a hard-pressed nation, continually goaded at its border and treated with contempt everywhere, began to rise.

The Constable of Harlech wrote to the Chamberlain of

Caernarfon, who in turn wrote to the King, that Welsh rebels were in touch with Scots from the 'Owt yles' (the Outer Isles) and that these were to land at Abermaw (Barmouth) to help the men of Merioneth rise. The Merioneth men were stealing horses and acquiring weapons; there were 'recheles men of divers countries' in wild Wales waiting to foment rebellion. Lord Grey of Ruthin was noticing similar murmurings in the northern Marches, and was anxious to be given greater powers to root out the troublemakers and deal with them. Strong measures were required, Grey noted, 'else trewly hitt will be an unruly Cuntrie within short time'. But King Henry had other problems on his mind. The time was ripe for the even more unruly Scots to be taught another lesson and he was raising an army for this purpose. He told his officers in Wales to offer pardons to anyone who had defied the law, in the hope that the dissatisfaction would die away.

Lord Grey was particularly bothered by the activities of Gruffydd ap Dafydd, a local bandit who had the temerity to steal the lord's horses. At the King's order, Gruffydd was offered a pardon and a position as a master forester, provided he gave himself up at Oswestry. He did so, and was lucky to escape alive. For many men the experience would have been a salutary lesson in dealing with the authorities but Gruffydd was aggrieved enough to confront Grey with his treachery in a letter. After a straightforward statement of the Oswestry betrayal he writes: 'I was told that you are in purpose to let your men burn and slay in any land which succours me and in which I am taken. Without doubt as many men as you slay for my sake and as many houses as you burn for my sake as many will I burn and slay for yours. And doubt not that I will have bread and ale of the best that is in your Lordship.'

It is a bold threat and earnestly meant, despite the gentlemanly close to the letter where Gruffydd ended, 'But God keep your worshipful estate in prosperity'!

Grey's face colour must have matched his name when he read the letter but in fact it was ammunition in his battle to increase his holding on the March. He sent a copy to the

Prince of Wales, Henry of Monmouth – later to become Henry
V of Agincourt – together with a copy of his reply to Gruffydd
in which he promised the Welshman, 'But we hoepe we shall
do thee a pryve thyng; a roope, a ladder, and a ryng, heigh
on gallowes for to henge. And thus shall be your endyng'.

It was a poetic ending and Grey must have felt the Fates
were on his side alone when they offered him Owain
Glyndwr. Henry IV was raising his army for Scotland in the
time-honoured fashion of calling for each noble to bring his
quota of men to the standard. Reginald Grey as chief Marcher
lord was given the task of passing on the summons to the
local nobles. Owain would have been asset to Henry, as a
proven fighting man with a knowledge of Scotland and the
Scots. His absence from the army so soon after Parliament
had ruled against him would have been badly taken. Grey
knew that, and somehow the summons was not passed on.

King Henry marched without Owain. His army was humil-
iated, a fact hardly likely to improve his temper, and he gave
leave to Grey to move against the treacherous Welshman. A
butt was needed for the royal anger and Owain would be that
butt. Grey knew that a straightforward attack would be
unlikely to capture the Welshman, who would escape long
before troops arrived, and that a show of force might provoke
hostility in his followers. He therefore arranged a meeting,
ostensibly to discuss Owain's problems; the latter agreed, but
limited the number of men to accompany Grey. Grey arrived
ostensibly with the small band stipulated, but a second group
secreted itself near the house to await a signal to attack. Iolo
Goch saw the ambush and, as he entertained hosts and guests
with a bardic poem, he told Owain of the planned attack in
cryptic verse. Owain left the room and escaped the house.
The long, luxurious autumn of his life at Sycharth was over.

On 16 September 1400 Owain was at Glyndyfrdwy, the
estate protected by the gorge of the Dee and its look-outs.
With him were his brother Tudor, from whom he could be
distinguished only by a wart under his left eye, other members
of his family and some close associates. A standard was raised

– the red dragon of Wales – and Owain was proclaimed Prince of Wales. Iolo Goch was there, and he sang a new song:

> Cambria's princely Eagle, hail,
> Of Gruffydd Vychan's noble blood,
> Thy high renown shall never fail,
> Owain Glyndwr, great and good,
> Lord of Dwrdwy's fertile Vale,
> Warlike high born Owain, hail!

In London four bells at the corners of a saintly shrine at Westminster rang of their own accord, not once but four times. A knell for the English king? – and in Wales the stream at Cilmery where the severed head of Llywelyn the Last had been washed, ran red all day. Blood, but whose?

Not unnaturally Owain decided to strike his first blow for Welsh independence against Grey at Ruthin. But if it is easy to see why Grey and Ruthin, it is less clear why he struck at all. What decided this dignified and cultured man to become a rebel at an age when most men of his time were content with heroic memories?

It is probable that at Glyndyfrdwy Owain received envoys from many Welsh families, pouring out their hatred for the Marcher lords and the English king. The generations of physical, emotional and economic suffering at the hands of the English had been polarized by the action of Henry IV against the pro-Welsh Richard, and by the contempt of Henry's Parliament for Owain, their highest born. A French knight at Henry's court said at the time of the investiture of young Prince Henry as Prince of Wales, that if the new prince were to have Wales he must conquer it, 'for in my opinion the Welsh would on no account allow him to be their lord, for the sorrow, evil and disgrace which the English, together with his father, had brought on King Richard'. Everyone but Henry and most of his lords failed to read the signs; those like Grey who did read them, played local, petty politics with the anger they betrayed.

The bards were spreading the word that freedom was at hand, that a hero had arisen. Owain was carried on the tide, perhaps. He must also have been looking for the restoration of his Sycharth estates, though a man need not be a prince to regain his land. Owain must have known that to take Sycharth was one thing but to hold it be quite another, and that the holding might require the creation of a free Wales.

On 18 September Owain's first army rode into Ruthin. The town was preparing for its fair, with stalls laid out and crowds gathering. The motley band of men that came through the town's gates were armed not only with swords and bows, but with sickles and rough-cut spears. In the shadow of Reginald Grey's red castle they fired the town and looted the market; the damage was estimated at £1,400, perhaps £250,000 in present-day terms. None of the townsfolk were killed but fourteen rebels were captured and Grey hanged them all.

Owain's band moved quickly. By 24 September they had fired and looted Denbigh, Flint, Hawarden, Holt, Rhuddlan and were advancing on Welshpool. But in the six days since the sacking of Ruthin, Hugh Burnell, Sheriff of Shrewsbury, had raised a small force from Shropshire, Staffordshire and Warwickshire and had marched to Welshpool. On the banks of the Vyrnwy Owain's band was routed, the men disappearing back to the valleys whence they had come.

The next day Henry and his army arrived in Shrewsbury. There he executed Goronwy ap Tudor, a kinsman of the Anglesey Tudors, a formidable family who had fought with King Richard. Goronwy's death was intended to encourage the others; his dismembered body was sent to Chester and Hereford, Ludlow and Bristol to encourage them even more.

The local rebellion has ended with the Vyrnwy defeat and the arrival of the royal army, but a second rebellion broke out in Anglesey led by Rhys and Gwilym ap Tudor, cousins of Owain. To quell it swiftly, Henry marched immediately to the island. All along the route the Welsh submitted to the King, but at Rhos Fawr near Beaumaris there was a sharp exchange with a band of Rhys Tudor's men. The Welsh retreated, then

Henry burned and looted the Franciscan house of Llanfaes Abbey before retreating in turn. He had sacked the house because the friars openly supported the rebels and because it was rich, the loot paying his mercenary soldiers.

Henry marched south through Gwynedd. He reached the Mawddwy on 13 October, then turned east and on 15 October arrived back in Shrewsbury. The country was peaceful. He offered a pardon to the leaders of the revolt and Tudor Glyndwr surrendered. But Owain was excepted from the pardon and his confiscated lands were given to John Beaufort, Earl of Somerset. The rebellion, it seemed, was over.

1401

In excepting Owain from the general pardon Henry IV had made a mistake, though he had placed himself in what might now be called a no-win position. If he pardoned Owain and returned his lands to him not only would he declare openly his inability to police Wales but would also publicly humiliate Reginald Grey who had started the whole episode. He would, however, placate Owain and maybe the Welsh. If, instead, he confiscated Owain's land, he would please Grey – though not as much as if he gave the land to him – and the English, but would antagonize Owain and maybe the Welsh. Henry took a calculated risk; it might have paid off, but he ensured it would not by allowing the English Parliament to enact a set of laws which were bound to evoke not merely antagonism but hatred in the Welsh.

It is not easy to understand why the Normans bothered the Welsh. The Saxons had pushed them back into their upland country and built Offa's Dyke at the point where it was decided to halt. Early conquests had been for land and for glory. The mineral wealth of Wales was not apparent a thousand years ago, and there was little glory in pursuing the warlike and hardy Celts into their hills where they could hide easily, appearing only to harass the invader and always cloaked in the vile mountain weather. The Marcher lords were, by law, allowed to take any land they could hold, and the 'Welsh dogs' were an easy source of self-aggrandizement, sport and loot. Small wonder the Welsh were angry; small wonder the English Parliament was contemptuous.

In early 1401 the contemptuous Parliament decided that no Welsh person could hold official office, or marry an English man or woman. The Welsh could not live in England and must pay for the damage done to English property in the rebellion of 1400.

Owain was still at Glyndyfrdwy, for although technically the estate had been confiscated it would have been a brave man who tried to enter the tight Dee valley and claim the land. But Gwynedd had accepted the royal pardon and Owain was isolated. By March 1401 he may well have had as few as seven followers, a few retainers. The situation was not good and without the new laws Owain might have sunk into obscurity. The savage legislation broke open the old wounds, however, though not there at Glyndyfrdwy but at Conwy.

On Good Friday the commander of Conwy Castle, John Massy, marched his garrison to church outside the castle walls. The castle, still one of the finest medieval buildings in Britain and a tribute to its builders, an almost perfect war machine, was left in the care of just two guards. Massy was an Englishman, well versed in the ways of European war. War in the early fifteenth century was a game played by kings and lords, moving their armies of peasants and mercenaries like chess pieces on the board of Europe. Like all good games there were rules, invented by the nobles and the church to avoid unholy behaviour, at least towards each other and not on Sunday. The Anglesey brothers Gwilym and Rhys ap Tudor were not bothered by these rules. With the garrison gone, two Welshmen approached the castle gate as carpenters, to carry out jobs inside. The two-man guard opened the gate to them and were killed immediately. Gwilym ap Tudor and forty of his men then fired Conwy and escaped into the castle.

By the time Massy had grasped what was going on the

town was burning beyond control, thousands of pounds' worth of damage had been done to English merchant property and the rebels were in control of the castle. Massy called the Chief Justice of North Wales to Conwy. The Chief Justice was Henry Percy, a man of thirty-five, the same age as the king, christened Hotspur by the Scots when he fought them on his sixteenth birthday. Hotspur was the son of the Earl of Northumberland who had helped to give Henry the crown, and was a favourite of the king. Knowing that Wales was a tinderbox and that Conwy could be the spark, he was anxious that the castle should be retaken quickly and wrote to the king asking for leave to offer a pardon to the rebels if they surrendered. There was no real alternative, for Conwy was so sound a fortress that only a long siege could hope to retake it if negotiations failed. The Tudors accepted the terms but King Henry did not. Again he could not win – to pardon the rebels would be to admit that no town in Wales was safe; to lay siege would allow Wales to realize his impotence. He decided not to sanction the pardons.

Negotiations dragged on for weeks. The Tudors could not hope to survive as there was no Welsh army large enough to relieve the castle from its blockade. Eventually a compromise was reached, one which reflected no credit on either side and appalled many even at a time in history when treachery and murder were commonplace. Nine of the rebels, selected by Gwilym ap Tudor, were taken while asleep and bound; then they were given over to the English in exchange for free passage for the remainder. Before Gwilym and the rest of his men were back in Anglesey, the nine had been drawn, hanged, disembowelled and quartered. Their butchered remains were sent about the country as a visible sign of the king's ruthless intentions towards all rebels.

What had been gained by this act? It is certain that the Tudors were acting independently of Owain, though their cause was similar. Excited by Owain's achievements they had joined in, perhaps not realizing the dire position in which they might be left as a result of this run up a blind alley. They can hardly have had much desire for rebellion after the appalling aftermath to their act. For Hotspur the end must have been equally unsatisfactory. He was a soldier not a barbarian, and butchering the nine rebels, while expedient, can have given him no satisfaction. By the end of May, Hotspur was disillusioned about his position in Wales. In letters to Henry he complains of lack of funds to pay his army and of his intention – unless things improve – of returning home. In reality he had no quarrel with the king over cash but was, rather, unhappy with Henry and, perhaps, unhappy with his treatment of Wales. Later Hotspur was to claim that he only wanted to help Henry regain the Lancaster lands, not to usurp Richard's crown. Later, too, he was to sign a treaty with Owain and in 1401 may even have had contact with the new Prince of Wales. Conwy may have been more of a victory than it seemed, however squalid.

As the spring of 1401 replaced the winter of 1400, the Welsh warmed gently to their new prince. At Oxford, always a favourite university with the Welsh, there were demonstrations in support of Welsh nationalism and many students returned home to fight for freedom. In England the Franciscans and many nobles, convinced that the Welsh revolt would return Richard to the throne, gave money to the cause. As much as £500,000 flowed across the border, though at some cost in human lives. One William Clark had his tongue pulled out for daring to speak against Henry, had his right hand cut off for daring to write against the king and was then beheaded, the final punishment certainly nullifying the effect of the other two but being, so the English thought, poetically savage. William Clark was not alone in his sacrifice.

By early May, with Conway Castle still occupied, Owain had collected some men together, though he was unfortunate when Hotspur encountered a group of them while he was showing the flag near Cadair Idris. Owain's small band was routed and, though the loss was hardly significant, he decided

Winter on Plynlimon

to move his summer operations to southern Wales.

Owain needed a mountain lair to which he could return and chose a secluded valley on the northern slopes of Plynlimon. There, near land that now lies beneath the waters of the Nant-y-moch reservoir, he raised his standard. A stone cairn and plaque now record the event. It was a symbolic gesture although the initial response was not overwhelming, the first army being just a few hundred strong. The band raided south and east, stealing food and cattle and burning houses; Llandrindod Wells, New Radnor and Montgomery were looted and fired.

Strangest of all, the abbey at Cwmhir was looted and burned. Beneath the turf of the abbey grounds the headless body of Llywelyn the Last lay interred and the abbey was a shrine to nationalism. But the Cistercian monks were believed to be in league with the English and so it was destroyed. It was the second time it had been razed, the first time having been by an English king who suspected the monks of Welsh sympathies. The true sympathy of the attackers in each case appears to have been with the abbey treasury. Owain's campaign had started to take on an unsavoury air.

Welshpool was attacked again but resisted stoutly and Owain's men withdrew to Plynlimon. There in the Hyddgen valley they rested, apparently unaware that an army was on the move towards them.

In south-east Wales there was a large body of immigrant Flemings, brought over by Henry I to boost the local woollen and craft industries. In time they had spread out, covering Pembrokeshire, Carmarthenshire and even southern Cardiganshire. In doing so they had displaced and antagonized the local Welsh, and any unruly behaviour among the natives could cost them dear. They decided, therefore, to take matters into their own hands and collected an army of 1500 to march north.

At Hyddgen – either because of excellent planning or appallingly slack defence by the Welsh, they succeeded in surrounding Owain with his band of about four hundred men. The Flemings had superiority in numbers, they had the element of surprise in their favour and the benefit of the terrain as they poured downhill into the valley and on to the trapped Welshmen. Owain and his men, facing inevitable defeat and knowing that capture meant death, fought with the fury of the desperate, halting and then reversing the Flemings' charge and finally putting them to flight. Owain's losses were few but the Flemings lost several hundred men. It was the first real battle of the war, not only won by the Welsh but in such a resounding way that loyal countrymen everywhere were cheered by the news and anxious to join the rebellion.

To mark the battle site two dazzling white calcite blocks were placed in the Hyddgen valley. The blocks were the Covenant Stones of Owain Glyndwr – named for a pilgrimage.

In June, Hotspur pulled his army out of north Wales and returned to Northumberland, and from then until September Owain's men ravaged the whole of Wales killing, burning and looting. The lands of the English were, as expected, the prime target but not all the Welsh were in sympathy with the rebellion. Those who were not found to their cost the price to be paid for failing to be enthused.

All summer King Henry waited, though why is not at all certain, but finally – when it seemed possible that Owain might actually invade England – he moved and on 8 October an English army arrived at Bangor. It marched to Caernarfon and turned south. The weather was excellent, the opposition non-existent and the king soon reached Strata Florida, an abbey south-east of Aberystwyth. The house was Cistercian, a brother abbey to Cwmhir, destroyed by Owain because the order was pro-English. At Strata Florida, King Henry's English army looted the abbey and stabled their horses in the nave.

Henry moved on towards Llandovery where a local squire, Llywelyn ap Gruffydd Vychan, promised to lead the army to Owain's hideout. For several days the squire led Henry about, until it became obvious that he was wasting their time and energy. Challenged, he admitted he had sons with Glyndwr and was leading the army astray. In Llandovery square, Llywelyn was butchered while King Henry watched. And in case such medicine might be good for the natives, other similar doses were meted out as the army fruitlessly sought its prey in mid-Wales. Owain's men made occasional forays to pick off outriders or to raid a baggage train, but would be away before any of Henry's main force arrived. The guerrilla tactics were successful but costly in civilian lives and liveli-hoods. Since the English could not batter the Welsh army, they battered the Welsh countryside.

Henry strengthened the garrison in the southern castles, feeling that in so doing he had subdued the area. In truth an Englishman was safe now only within his massive stone walls, and to make the point clearly Owain attacked Caernarfon in November and Harlech in December. Neither attack was successful – indeed the Caernarfon attack cost many lives – nor was it expected to be, but it had the desired effect of keeping English heads down while the Welsh bands con-tinued their round of looting and burning.

Despite his successes, Owain knew that he had little real chance against the English unless he could gain more support. He might have the majority of the Welsh on his side, but Henry had the professional army and the castles. In an effort to obtain more support Owain wrote to Scotland and Ireland, noting their common ancestry and the prophecies which told that with their help Owain would rid the countryside for good of their 'mortal enemies, the Saxons'. The letters, written in French, are in the convoluted form of the time but clearly written by a man capable of pinpointing the likely features that would best draw support from cousin Celts. They are also notable for the form and frequency of the address to the King of Scotland – 'redoubted lord and Sovereign Cousin' and the King of Ireland – 'dread lord and most trusty Cousin'. Owain was not only a fine general but an astute politician.

He was certainly astute enough to hedge his bet on the likelihood of gaining support and total victory. Through the Northumberland Percys he entered into a peace negotiation with Henry. The king was inclined to accept; Owain wanted only the return of his estates and a pardon for himself and this time it would not be unreasonable to accede. Henry was hard pressed in Wales and peace at any cost might be better than having to continue fighting and, probably, to continue failing to protect the English in Wales. A nice face-saving withdrawal on both sides seemed to suit everyone. But it did not suit Grey, who hated Glyndwr, or Beaufort, who wanted Glyndwr's estates. In the end it was decided to use peace talks as a means of capturing Owain, but to his great credit Percy would have none of this.

So the die was cast. Since Henry would not be allowed to make peace, he and Owain would have to make war. It was probably a decision that both men feared and regretted. By the end of 1401, a year that had started so badly for Owain seemed to be ending well, but it is doubtful whether Owain was thrilled with the prospects for 1402.

1402

In February a comet crossed the sky, 'a terror to the world', and a cause of some excitement and much outright fear in the superstitious peasant classes of Europe. Iolo Goch saw the comet as a sign. Such a fiery star had been seen when Arthur had been born, and there had also been one above Bethlehem. The portent was clear – Owain was a warrior-king and saviour. As if to prove the point the comet, when seen from England, pointed towards Wales, and on occasions curled its tail and took on the shape of a dragon.

England and Wales were struck by violent thunderstorms, lightning tearing the sky apart. At one English church, lightning struck the roof and half demolished the building. The terrified congregation had no time to escape before the Devil came in, dressed as a Franciscan monk, one of the order who sided with Owain. He jumped over the altar and fled again, passing so close to one man that the man's legs were blackened for all time, as if from fire. The smell of sulphur took everyone's breath.

As if to prove the omens correct – though who would deny them in any event? – as the comet was heading into the Welsh sky, Owain captured his greatest enemy, Reginald Grey. It seems that on 31 January Owain appeared before Ruthin, challenging Grey to a fight. Then, or so one story has it, Owain shod his horses backwards so that Grey believed his cavalry had retreated. Grey charged the few remaining infantry only to discover that they were merely helmets set on top of poles. Too late he realized his mistake, as the Welsh poured out from woodland on his flanks to hack his men to pieces. Other stories suggest that Grey's own men had betrayed him, through love either of Owain or of the bribe he offered them. Either way the day ended with the Lord of Ruthin, trussed up and obscene with anger, being taken to a makeshift prison either at Llansantffraid in Powys, or in Snowdonia. No one man can ever be held responsible for a war that lasts half a generation; there must be others who help him, knowingly or by stupidity in default. But the Glyndwr rebellion was started by Reginald Grey, and it is likely that it continued beyond the winter of 1401 because of his efforts to ensure it was prolonged. His capture was poetic justice.

Grey was immediately ransomed. Though Owain had cause to hate this man who had sought to humiliate him and had actually stolen his lands and made him an outlaw, butchery was out of the question. Grey was worth a lot of money. To be exact he was worth £10,000, the bulk to be paid in one month. Grey would then be replaced by his son who would stand surety for the rest. In fact the colossal sum took months to produce and its collection ruined Grey financially as his lands were sold to raise some of the cash. He had started the war to make a financial killing; he ended it in penury. Moreover, whereas by his actions he would have liked to see Glyndwr dead, he survived only by Owain's clemency and had to sign an agreement never to raise a sword against him again.

Although the omens and the capture of Grey raised Welsh morale, and convinced many that Owain was indeed Celtic Freedom reborn, there were others who were unconvinced. Owain's cousin, Hywel Sele of Nannau near Dolgellau, was not convinced that the rebellion was correct. In an attempt to smooth things over the Abbot of Cymer Abbey, near Nannau, persuaded the two men to meet and they walked on Hywel's estate with Hywel carrying his bow. When a deer was started Hywel fitted an arrow – aiming and firing not at the deer but at Owain, whose life was saved because he was wearing a mail coat below his jerkin. Hywel was never seen again, but forty years later a great oak split and inside its hollow centre was found the skeleton of a man. Owain had killed Hywel and concealed his body in *ceubren yr ellyll*, the hollow tree of a fiend. The troubled spirit of Hywel haunted the area, and the Haunted Oak was shunned until it was destroyed by lightning four hundred years later.

Elsewhere in Wales, Owain had little to fear. True the great castles were still in English hands but castles were a strange war engine. In our days of enhanced mobility it is difficult to understand how a castle could be of any use. True it protected its inhabitants very well but why not just walk around it? Or sit outside and wait for the garrison to die of starvation? The truth is that the castle's worth can only be understood in the context of medieval warfare, when to keep a huge army in the field was a prodigious logistical feat. The supply lines had to be maintained – leave a castle untaken and as you moved on its garrison came out behind you to chop off your umbilical cord. Sit around it – and the cost of doing nothing could mean insolvency.

However, in 1402 Wales was largely Owain's; he had no supply lines to protect, he had all the time in the world. The castles were symbolic of a power that had retreated from the fray.

In England, King Henry was closing his mind to the Welsh problem. He had not won the crown merely to fiddle about with the Scots, Irish and Welsh; he wanted a crusade to win

The battlefield, Pilleth

him glory and everlasting salvation. It was a fine dream but one about to be rudely shattered.

In spring and early summer Owain devastated north Wales. Significantly he left Denbigh, Hotspur's estate, alone and moved southward towards Powys. By June he was approaching the land of the Mortimers. Edmund Mortimer was uncle of the Earl of March who, as a direct descendant of Edward III and the named heir of Richard II, had a greater claim on the English throne than the usurper Henry. The existence of the young earl was of concern to Henry who obviously did not feel strong enough to dispose of him, but wanted him well-guarded in case he became the focus of anti-Lancastrian feelings. Edmund, the boy's protector, mustered an army of several thousand and marched to meet the Welsh.

At Pilleth, a hamlet near Knighton, Owain's men at long last stood their ground on the ridge of the steep slope of Bryn Glas – next to the present beautiful church, not in the valley as sited by the Ordnance Survey. Edmund would not attack up the slope; that would have been ludicrous. But that is what he ordered his men to do. His Herefordshire-levied troops with English knights in support charged, and as they did Mortimer's Welsh archers poured arrows into them, apparently in an act of spontaneous support for Owain. The English army – to be precise, the English part of Mortimer's army – was slaughtered.

When it was all over, and it would not have taken long, the Welsh stayed on their ridge above the huge pile of dead. Estimates vary but there were probably between one and two thousand men stretched out on the slopes. Owain's men were accompanied by what was for those times the normal entourage of women – camp-followers, wives, cooks and so on. 'After the batayle ful shamefully the Walsch women cutte off mennes membris and put hm in here mouthis.'

And: 'The shameful villany used by the Welsh women towards the dead carcasses was such as honest ears would be ashamed to hear and continent tongues to speak thereof. The dead bodies might not be buried without great sums of money being given for liberty to convey them away.'

And again: 'A thousand . . . butchered; upon whose dead corpses there was much misuse, such beastly shameless transformation by those Welshwomen done as may not be without much shame retold or spoken of.'

The English dead were mutilated and then the bodies were sold to the grieving relatives. Many were not claimed and only a century ago a farmer ploughing Bryn Glas uncovered the heaped bones of the rest. They were re-interred and a clump of fir trees planted on the spot. Today these trees stand tall against hill and sky.

The stories of the aftermath of the battle may have been exaggerated: propaganda is not a new weapon. But there is

Pilleth church

probably a grain of truth. Owain's campaigns had been bloody, but then the times were bloody – the English had invented the 'scorched earth' policy in France to frighten the natives into submission, to reduce their will and ability to fight back. At Pilleth the pent-up hatred of years of effective slavery were vented in one vile outrage.

So what is the true story of the Bryn Glas battle? Later writers have made much of the tactics employed by Rhys Gethin, Owain's lieutenant, in taking up a position beyond the ridge and so effectively ambushing from behind the hill, a very advanced technique. But if Rhys the Fierce was so good, why was Pilleth so rare as a pitched battle? There were probably only 4,000 Welsh there, but Henry's armies apart, that was a considerable force in Wales during the rebellion. And what of the Welsh archers changing sides?

King Henry thought he knew the answer and accused Mortimer – himself captured in the fight – of treason. Later events do suggest that Mortimer was anti-Henry and he did become surprisingly pro-Glyndwr in a short space of time. Also, of course, Hotspur was his brother-in-law.

Owain demanded a ransom for Mortimer which Henry refused to pay. Hotspur was furious: how could the king pay for Grey and refuse to pay for Mortimer? A chronicler of the time reports a face-to-face confrontation, with Henry touching his sword and Hotspur shouting, 'Not here, but on the field of battle'. And Hotspur returned to Northumberland.

With Mortimer's men destroyed, Owain swept south, destroying Abergavenny and Cardiff and sacking the bishop's palace beside Llandaff Cathedral. He also maintained his blockade on Caernarfon and Harlech castles, and now besieged Criccieth.

King Henry was troubled. Four thousand Scots were massing on the northern border and he could not count on Hotspur. He needed a quick victory in Wales or his kingdom could well be in ruins by year's end. In late August he massed 100,000 men on the Welsh border, in three separate armies, and in early September he invaded Wales.

For several years the bards had been telling the people that Owain was supernatural. Now, with a vast army in their country, the people needed a sign and Owain needed to show his ability at 'calling spirits from the vasty deep'. As Henry's three armies advanced, the weather changed and for fourteen successive days the rain lashed down on his men, driven sometimes by fierce winds. The rivers rose and became impassable. The men had no shelter and slept in chilling rain. The supplies were destroyed by water. Henry's tent was thrown down by a storm and he survived only because he was still in armour. In mid-September the armies retreated, men dying of exposure along the roads back to England. The invasion was over, no sight or sound of Owain had been seen.

All was hidden behind his magician's cloak of weather!

The English soldiers – without hot food for days, chilled and sodden wet, frightened by the storms and by the knowledge that unseen Welshmen were picking off stragglers – knew now that Owain could command the elements. 'Through art magicke as was thought, he [Owain] caused much foul weather of windes, tempests, rain, snow and hail to be raised for the annoyance of the King's army, the like of which had never been seen.'

In Shakespeare's *Henry IV*, Part One Owain says:

> Three times hath Henry Bolingbroke made head
> Against my power. Thrice from the banks of Wye
> And sandy-bottomed Severn have I sent
> Him bootless home, and weather beaten back.

And he had a stone that a raven had spat out for him, which made him invisible. How could anyone fight such a man?

1403

Towards the end of 1402 two events, widely separated in space if not in time, gave heart to both sides. In Wales Edmund Mortimer married Owain's daughter, Jane, thus ensuring a pact between the Welsh prince and a possible English king, the Earl of March. Edmund wrote to his estate manager:

> I greet you much and make known to you that Oweyn [*sic*] Glyndwr has raised a quarrel of which the object is, if King Richard be alive, to restore him to his crown; and if not that, my honoured nephew, who is the right heir to the said crown shall be king of England, and that the said Oweyn will assert his right in Wales. And I, seeing and considering that the said quarrel is good and reasonable, have consented to join in it, and to aid and maintain it, and by the grace of God to a good end. Amen.

But in the north, at Homildon, Hotspur defeated the Scottish army; he captured its leader, the Earl of Douglas, and freed King Henry from immediate fears of invasion.

The allegiance with a possible new English king was good but before Owain could consider or assist in invading England, he had first to secure Wales. South-west Wales, the land of the Flemings – still smarting from the Hyddgen defeat – had to be taken. To that end Owain campaigned south and west, though he still maintained the siege of the northern castles. Letters written by the constables of Dinefwr and Brecon castles, who were brothers, allow us a first-hand glimpse of conditions at the time. They talk of Owain with eight thousand lances at his back, dominating the area with his feared lieutenants – Rhys Gethin the Fierce, Rhys Ddu and Rhys the son of Llywelyn from Llandovery who died for misleading the royal army. From Dinefwr comes: 'There is great peril for me for they have made a vow that they will all have us ded therin; wherfor I pray thee that thou wilt not boggle us, but send to us a warning within a short time whether we schule have any help or no.'

The king too, was made aware of these cries for help. From Brecon came:

. . . to ordain thereupon speedy remedy for the destruction and resistance of the rebels in those parts of South Wales, who are treacherously raised against you and your Majesty, so that your castles and towns and the faithful men in them be not thus ruined and destroyed for lack of aid and succour. And besides, may it please your lordship to know that the rebels . . . are lying near the town of Brecon doing all the mischief they can to its town and neighbourhood, and they purpose, all of them together, to burn all pertaining to the English in the same parts if they be not resisted in haste.

The message from Hereford was: '. . . the whole country is lost unless you go there as quick as possible. Be pleased to set forth with all your power and march by night as well as by day, for the salvation of those parts.'

It is clear that in every part of Wales Owain's men were in command outside the castle walls. But he did not have it all his own way. In early July Owain halted his thrust into the Fleming land of Pembrokeshire at Laugharne, later to become a place of pilgrimage for those seeking the Welshman as poet. He wanted to talk to Lord Thomas Carew, who held the castle there. Several local castles had fallen easily; Owain was hoping for another, and probably feared a direct fight with the Flemings who were difficult adversaries, despite their poor showing at Hyddgen. As talks progressed a band of Welshmen slipped quietly around the side of the castle, taking a hillside route to avoid detection. But Carew was a wily foe and his men, set in the hills in readiness for just such a move, ambushed the band of seven hundred men. Not one escaped.

To make things worse a local seer, Hopkin ap Thomas, told Owain that he would be captured and dragged away beneath a black banner, on the Gower. Owain had set great store by the bardic prophecies on his behalf and while it is idle to discuss whether he actually believed it all, it is obvious from the fact that he consulted the seer that he would have to take heed of his advice. Some have suggested that Hopkin made his prophecy in order to protect the Gower. Whether that is true or not Owain retreated from the area and back towards Carmarthen.

While his thrust into south-west Wales was being halted by the defeat at Laugharne, news was arriving of the destruction of his estates at Sycharth and Glyndyfrdwy. The attacks were undoubtedly upsetting for Owain, though he may have consoled himself with the knowledge that he was now acting out his life on a wider stage. What was of greater significance, though it could hardly have been realized at the time, was that the leader of the English force was the other Prince of Wales, Henry of the cry 'God for Harry, England and St George!' at Agincourt. That battle would be won by a leader trained in the rugged terrain of Wales. Now he was just a boy but he was a good learner as time would tell.

While Owain was stopped at Laugharne, King Henry was raising an army in England. He had received the letters from Wales begging him to help the beleaguered fortresses, and others from his son saying that the retainers in the northern Marches were deserting for lack of pay. It would be natural therefore to assume that he was preparing an invasion of Wales. Such an assumption would be quite wrong. In fact Henry was preparing to invade Scotland!

At this remove in time it is difficult to comprehend the almost blind recklessness of such a move. To the west the Welsh were threatening to invade England, while the Scots occupied a country filled with a people both poor and consumed with hate for their southern neighbours. Of course, in view of the history of the Welsh, apparently borne out by subsequent events, it could be that Henry was cleverer than he appears.

It is likely that even as Henry was preparing his Scottish army, news reached him that was to have a direct bearing on the outcome of Owain's rebellion, even though it concerned only Englishmen in England. Following the Homildon battle Hotspur ransomed his prisoners, including the Earl of Douglas, after the time-honoured fashion. Such high-born captives were spoils of war. But Henry demanded the prisoners – and thus by implication the ransom – for himself. For Hotspur this was the last straw. First Mortimer had been refused ransom and now Henry wanted his prisoners. Having already had talks with Owain and Edmund Mortimer, the Percys decided to break with the king. The old Earl of Northumberland was ill but Hotspur, eager as always to be on the move, departed immediately towards Wales. At Chester he formed an army, mostly untrained but with troops of the now-friendly Earl of Douglas – glad just to be allowed to kill Englishmen! – and the Chester longbowmen, feared everywhere.

On 20 July Hotspur's army approached Shrewsbury. To his horror the town was occupied not by a small royal garrison or – much better (and expected?) – by Owain's men, but by the king, who had shown an absolute mastery in the art of forming and force-marching an army. Thirty thousand troops were waiting for Hotspur's fifteen thousand men, and to add to Hotspur's misery, he discovered that the hamlet where he had to spend the night was called Berwick. Long ago a seer had told him he would die in Berwick and he had assumed this would be in a border war with the Scots; now he saw it was to be in civil war with the English king. In despair he said, 'I perceive my plough is now drawing to its last furrow.'

Despite the despair, on 21 July at a site now called Battle-field, five kilometres north-east of Shrewsbury centre, Hot-spur commanded with his usual flair. His Chester archers slaughtered the king's bowmen and created havoc in the ranks of his knights. Only when Douglas, inflamed by the sight of all those Englishmen in disarray, charged, nullifying the archers' effect, did the tide turn. The fifteen-year-old Henry of Monmouth turned Hotspur's flank, receiving a face wound for his efforts. Confusion reigned, but when it cleared Hotspur himself was dead, his army defeated.

After the battle Hotspur was buried close to the field, along with at least four thousand of his friends and foes. But Henry would not settle for that. Too often the Welsh had placed their faith in princes who had disappeared but, they said, would appear again when the time was right. Henry wanted to deny them this hope, however vain it was, and had Hotspur's body dug up and exhibited in Shrewsbury market-place, so that everyone could see that he really was dead. For good measure the body was quartered and distributed; the head went to a spike on York town gates. A church was built over the mass grave, the only church in England that is a war memorial.

Had Hotspur won history would have been so different as to be beyond computing. Had he reached Owain then Wales would have won its freedom – at least until Mortimer or Northumberland chose otherwise. So why was Owain not at Shrewsbury? Henry called him a coward, and a tale arose that Owain watched the slaughter from an oak tree, afraid of pitched battles. That is unlikely. It is more likely that Hot-spur's impetuosity cost him and Owain victory; that and poor

communications. If Hotspur had awaited his father's better
health he would have had a bigger force and given Owain time
to extricate himself from the problems at Laugharne. Or had
word reached Owain in time, he might have made it to the field.

Two things are clear. The first is that Hotspur underesti-
mated the king's logistical ability and his son's fighting
qualities. The second is that the Welsh were betrayed by the
nature of their campaign. Had they taken and held Shrewsbury then the battle would have gone to the allies. The strike-
and-run guerrilla warfare was winning battles but it was not
winning the war.

From Shrewsbury the king marched north to quell an
incipient rising in Northumberland. The old earl, sick and
sorrowful, rode through York's gates with his king, past the
blackening head of his son, and came to heel.

In Wales Owain continued to cut a swaithe across the land,
apparently oblivious of Shrewsbury and its implication. He
invaded Herefordshire, dragging legislation out of Henry that
any Welshman found in any border town would be executed.
The situation for the beleaguered English worsened and on 15
September Henry invaded Wales for the fourth time. He
marched to Carmarthen, issuing orders, proclamations and
pardons without number. He then turned and marched out
again. It had taken four days and achieved nothing. No rebels
were seen, let alone engaged, and within a day or two of his
departure from Wales Owain was in Glamorgan taking Cardiff, Caerphilly, Newport, Usk and Caerleon.

Owain now had at least ten thousand men at arms, perhaps
as many as thirty thousand and, in addition, he was receiving
some small assistance from the French. Chiefly this involved
piracy on the southern English coast, actions guaranteed to
keep English soliders out of Wales, but there was a landing of
troops in Carmarthen and Breton soldiers were assisting at
the siege of Caernarfon.

Ignoring Shrewsbury as being an English affair, it had been
a good year for the Welsh. Optimism ran high as winter
brought 1403 to an end.

1404

In early 1404 Owain was so secure in Wales that he could concentrate his efforts on the remaining strongholds, the castles of north Wales. The records that are preserved show just how impregnable the great castles were when defended by able and courageous men – but conversely just how useless they were, except as symbols, if the occupiers did not control the surrounding country. At Caernarfon twenty-eight men were holding the castle against the combined efforts of Owain and his small squadron of French allies. To visit Caernarfon castle now, with its museum of recent Prince of Wales regalia, its well-tended lawns and the hustle of visitors, is to be impressed by the scale and immense beauty of the structure. In January 1404 these twenty-eight men kept watch on those towers and battlements, forever watchful and fearful of another attempt to scale their walls. Henry IV had forgotten them. They watched, hour after hour, ticking off the hours to when they would die of starvation if Owain did not reach them first. That is true bravery, not the valorous act of desperate men in the alien situation of battle, but the day-long, night-long courage of men in a normal, yet extraordinarily abnormal, situation.

At Harlech, south of Caernarfon, perched on a rock outcrop between the sea of Cardigan Bay and the unremitting rocks of the Rhinogs, the men broke. Owain badly wanted one of these great castles and, it is thought that by offering bribes or pardons to the beleaguered garrison, he won Harlech. When the gates were finally opened to the Welsh there were sixteen men left. Of all the castles this was the one which raised Welsh hearts; it was here that Bran the Blessed had had his rocky fortress and the site was Welsh back to pre-history.

Harlech was no Sycharth; it was harsh and cold where Sycharth had been lush and friendly. But to the castle Owain brought his family, and if it did not suit his wife and children it enraptured Iolo Goch. A Welsh Prince of Wales and at an ancestral place!

Here is the life I've sighted for long
Abashed is now the Saxon throng
And Britons have a British Lord
Whose emblem is the conquering sword . . .

He extolled Owain, the hero of the watery dell, the bloody
spear in field. The spear would be bloodier yet, but who could
deny the old bard what he had waited a lifetime to see?

Grace, wisdom, valour, all are thine,
Owain Glyndowerdy divine,
Meet emblem of a two-edged sword,
Dreaded in war, in peace adored.

Loud fame has told thy gallant deeds,
In every word a Saxon bleeds,
Terror and flight together came,
Obedient to thy mighty name;
Death in the van with ample stride
Hew'd thee a passage deep and wide . . .

In the wake of Harlech, Criccieth and Aberystwyth fell and
now Owain was in control of Wales from coast to coast. So
secure was his position that he could stop being solely a
warrior king and start to be a statesman. He called a parliament at Machynlleth, a convenient spot to gather together
'few persons of sufficient consequence' from every cantref of
ancient Wales. Today the site of this first Welsh parliament
house holds an ancient, though not sufficiently ancient, dour
stone building with a simple inscription.

The parliament was a regal occasion but again death was in
the van. Dafydd ap Llywelyn ap Hywel, known as Davy Gam
– 'gam' from crooked, because he had squint eyes – came
from Brecon. He was red-haired and long-armed, a man of
quick temper who had fled Brecon at a young age after killing
a neighbour. At Machynlleth he tried to kill Owain, probably
as a service for Henry Bolingbroke whom he had known from
childhood; when he fled Brecon he had joined the service of

Memorial plaque to Glyndwr's parliament, Machynlleth

John of Gaunt.

Gam's plot was discovered but surprisingly, in view of the treatement Hywel Sele had received, Owain did not kill him. This has often been ascribed to Gam's being a relative but that is not the case. It was another Gam who was a relative – and Hywel Sele was in any case a cousin. The reason for the clemency is not known, although another theory is that such an act might have been made to project Owain as a magnanimous ruler. Equally, it might have been to ensure that Gam rotted away nastily in a damp dungeon somewhere. In fact Gam was eventually released and fought and died for Bolingbroke's son at Agincourt. He was knighted as he died,

winning fame for his often quoted reply when his king asked
how many French there were: 'Enough to kill, to take prisoner
and to run away'. He is widely believed to have been the
model for Fluellen, Shakespeare's all-encompassing Welshman – though that name is clearly an English attempt to spell
Llywelyn. It is an irony that this Welshman of all of them
should be so honoured.

Although he did not kill Gam, Owain destroyed his estates
at Brecon. It is said that the cultured Owain even lapsed into
verse over the incident, telling Gam's bailiff:

> Canst thou a little red man descry,
> Looking around for his dwelling fair?
> Tell him it under the bank doth lie,
> And its brow the mark of a coal doth bear.

At Machynlleth Owain may have been crowned again. Certainly he took a royal coat of arms; significantly it was not the
lion of Powys, despite his descent from that line, but the four
lions of Gwynedd, the ancient warrior kingdom. There were
representatives from France and Spain at Machynlleth and
gifts were brought for the new ruler. He appointed a Chancel-
lor, Gruffydd Young, and sent him and his brother-in-law
John Hanmer to France to negotiate a formal treaty of
allegiance.

Not everyone was impressed by this show of government
and Adam of Usk wrote: 'Owen and his hill-men . . . held or
counterfeited or made pretence of holding parliaments.' But
despite Adam another parliament followed at Dolgellau and
Owain's forces moved towards the English border. The French
treaty was signed at Aberystwyth and the French prepared a
fleet to sail to Wales. In its ships would be an army for the
invasion of England.

Owain's forces again ravaged Herefordshire but once more
stopped at the border. The panic over probable invasion was
now such that beacon fires were prepared to signal its occur-
rence and Prince Henry of Monmouth wrote in great alarm to

On the Way near Machynlleth

his 'most dread and sovereign lord and father'. The plea fell on deaf ears, King Henry did nothing either to reinforce or relieve the beleaguered castles of north Wales, or to bolster the defences of the Marches.

Richard Beauchamp, the young Earl of Warwick, was less complacent – or more probably less hard-pressed financially – and decided that the Severn was as far as he wanted Owain to advance. In June he crossed the river with a large force, in search of the small army that had now turned south toward Glamorgan. At Campstone Hill, about 5 kilometres south-west of Grosmont Castle, Beauchamp found his quarry and there was a fierce battle in which Owain's standard was captured. Remarkably, Owain himself was almost captured –

what was he doing here so close to the English border, so far from Harlech? We shall soon see.

The defeat was a bitter turn of events, for it suggested again that the Welsh were no match for a disciplined English army. Perhaps sensing that the result could damage Welsh morale, Owain re-grouped and pursued the English who unwisely had not chased the Welsh after they broke at Campstone. At Craig-y-dorth, about 5 kilometres south-east of Monmouth, he caught them, beat them soundly in a running battle and, to make the point, chased them back to Monmouth town.

In August Owain was in Cardiff. In fact his decision to be there was why he was so nearly captured at Campstone, and why he had therefore been available to restore Welsh pride at Monmouth. The reason for his presence at Cardiff lay in the English Channel, for that month a fleet of sixty vessels had sailed from Harfleur to land an army in Wales for the invasion of England. The fleet was under the Count of March, and every day Welsh soldiers lined the Glamorgan coast waiting for it to appear over the horizon. They waited in vain. Whether by orders or on his own (non-) initiative, the count sailed up and down the English Channel pretending to be an invasion fleet. He succeeded in frightening the south coast towns, but he failed to frighten Henry IV who ignored him as he ignored Owain. Again the king was proved right. Owain's men became sore-eyed in vain. In November the count returned his fleet to Harfleur: he had not landed any troops anywhere.

By November Owain too had retreated, back to his castle stronghold at Harlech. Despite the lack of real activity in the showy procession of the Count of March's fleet, the treaty with the French was ratified. In addition, several treaties were made with English border provinces. Edward de Charleton, the Lord of Powys, made a truce from his Red Castle, at a cost of course. And so did the people of Shropshire. Theirs was the more important treaty, for it guaranteed their peace – again at a price – for three months, not from rebels to the English crown but from the 'Land of Wales'.

1405

Early in 1405 there was a plot to release the young Earl of
March, the true heir to the English throne, from the benign –
for the moment – but steady grip of King Henry. Some
authorities claim that the Tri-partite Indenture signed between
Northumberland, Mortimer and Owain was drawn up at this
time, and that the plot was necessary for the treaty, the
signatories needing a figure-head for their cause. In general,
however, it is believed that the treaty was signed in 1406 and
that the plot was an independent scheme – and it is that
sequence that is followed here.

The young earl and his brother were at Windsor for the
Christmas of 1404, in the charge of Lady Despencer, while the
king and his court were elsewhere. A small party including
Lady Despencer and the boys left Windsor as the new year
dawned, and made haste westward. It was required only that
they crossed the Severn, for once in Wales there was no hope
for the survival of any pursuing band. It is believed that
Henry heard of the escape while the party was still in
Berkshire and a desperate chase began. The earl's party
reached the border of Gloucestershire. The safety of the
Severn was only a day away now – but it was one day too far,
as they were caught by Henry's men.

Lady Despencer, in fear of her life, claimed her action was
part of her brother's plot to kill the king, and also told the
name of the locksmith who had made her the keys she had
used for the escape. Her brother, the Duke of York, denied
the charge, and was eventually pardoned. The locksmith had
his hands cut off. Such was the justice of medieval England.

Whether this abortive rescue mission occurred before or
after the signing of the Tri-partite Indenture, it was another
blow to Welsh hopes though again, as after Shrewsbury,
Owain's men continued as before. Rhys Gethin, that loyal
lieutenant, collected an army of eight thousand men and
moved into Monmouthshire. Again there were fears that
England was to be invaded, and Prince Henry decided to

make a stand. Throughout the years of Welsh dominance the young prince, still only eighteen, had steadfastly refused to ignore the Welsh rebellion. Now, it seems, he had decided that even if his father was happy with the situation west of the Severn, he was not. At Grosmont Castle he collected a small army of fine soldiers and waited.

Rhys arrived at Grosmont and burnt it to the ground. But Welsh joy was shortlived, for Prince Henry emerged from the castle and forced them to stand and fight. After the battle the prince wrote to his father:

> My most redoubted and most Sovereign lord and father . . . your people gained the field, and vanquished all the said rebels, and slew of them by fair account in field, by the time of their return from the pursuit, some say eight hundred, others a thousand, being questioned upon pain of death.

The engagement had been a disaster for the Welsh. There were Welsh archers on Prince Henry's side and they remained loyal, inflicting terrible damage on the army of Rhys. Owain was greatly concerned by the defeat and immediately sent his brother Tudor to regroup the local force. Owain's son, Gruffydd, arrived to join Tudor and they prepared to attack the castle at Usk to which Prince Henry had moved. The Abbot of Llantarnam Abbey celebrated a mass for the soldiers, who were told that those who died bravely would that night 'sup in heaven'. There were men who would find out if he was correct.

The Welsh attacked the castle and Prince Henry again opened the gates and charged out, breaking the Welsh ranks and scattering the army in confusion. The Welsh fled east to Mynydd Pwll Melyn, the Hill of the Yellow Pool, less than 3 kilometres from Usk. There Tudor and Gruffydd attempted to form a battle-line, but Prince Henry was a new enemy. He did not fight and wait, he fought and chased. The Welsh lines were not complete before the prince arrived to break them. The Welsh ran into the woods – called Coed y Pwll-Llyn by the Ordnance Survey in an elegant misrendering of Welsh – and were relentlessly pursued, hacked down or captured. Tudor Glyndwr was killed and jubilation ran through the English until the lack of a wart under the left eye showed he was not Owain. The Abbot of Llantarnam was also dead as were many, many more. Gruffydd, roped to his captive men, was led back to Usk where, to encourage the men of south Wales, three hundred prisoners were beheaded. Gruffydd was spared, if being imprisoned in the Tower is being spared. In appalling conditions he survived six years, dying eventually of disease.

Adam of Usk wrote of this battle in his home town, where the English nobles 'slew with fire and the edge of the sword many of them without ceasing'. Gruffydd, he noted, was 'cut off by pestilence'.

The remnants of the shattered army edged back towards north Wales. When one soldier asked another abbot who had helped at the mass before Usk why he had not stayed to sup in heaven, the abbot replied that it was one of his fast days.

In the wake of Grosmont and Usk, King Henry, shrewd as ever, offered pardon to all who renounced the rebellion and virtually the whole of south-east Wales responded to his call. Realizing that the time had come to reinforce the Welsh change of heart by advancing into mid- or north Wales, Henry gathered an army of forty thousand men on the border at Hereford. To add to Owain's problems the safe island of Anglesey was lost when Beaumaris Castle was retaken by the crown. The situation looked desperate: it was clear that a summer invasion of mid-Wales would inevitably lead to more defections to Henry, and equally clear that after the reverses at Grosmont and Usk, Owain's army could not hope to stand and fight. What Owain needed was time, and to obtain that he required a diversion.

Whether by happy chance, or by chance assisted by his own councillors in Northumberland, the north of England now rose in revolt under Richard Scrope, Archbishop of York. As usual, Henry saw any other rebellion as being more serious than that in Wales, and immediately moved his army north-ward. At Shipton Moor in Yorkshire the revolt was put down and Scrope was captured and butchered. Also executed was one of Owain's ambassadors to Northumberland. It is still not clear whether Owain fuelled the rebellion, or whether the north saw the chance to rise because Henry was pre-occupied in Wales.

Henry stayed through the summer maintaining the peace in the north, and Owain used the time well, allowing his battered men time to recover, strengthening the morale of the wavering parts of his principality and then, in late July, gathering ten thousand men in Pembrokeshire to await another French invasion fleet. The French put to sea with 140 ships, but this time the weather would not allow them to parade in the channel. To the unrelieved joy of the Welsh the seas drove the French, not homeward, but to Milford Haven. The French army disembarked, together with its leader Robert of the One Eye, but with none of the horses all of which had died of thirst on the crossing.

Estimates of the size of the French force vary but it was probably around five thousand in total. They joined Owain's army and the combined force marched on Haverfordwest, which was razed. The castle was not taken and to express their displeasure the Welsh slaughtered the citizens of this English and Fleming township. Next, Tenby received the same treatment. At this stage it appears that the French would like to have gone home; however, an English fleet under Lord Berkeley arrived, sinking many ships at anchor, and the French were marooned. That many pressed men are needed to replace one volunteer is proverbial, and with his mixture of both Owain marched on Carmarthen. The town surrendered and next Glamorgan was punished for accepting the royal pardon. Owain was again in control of Wales.

Now, for the first and only time, in mid-August 1405, Owain invaded England. It was three and a half centuries since England had last been invaded by a foreign power in numbers sufficient to cause alarm. King Henry, despite his war-weariness after five years of endless struggle, and his near-bankruptcy, hurried to Worcester to face the invaders who were camped on nearby Woodbury Hill. The chosen camp site was indicative of Owain's indecision at this time. It was a beautiful defensive position, but what had he to defend? He could hope neither to conquer England from a defensive camp, nor to feed his men indefinitely here in hostile England. But Owain feared pitched battles with the English, which may have been his reason for staying at Woodbury. If that was the case he would have been better retreating, for it can have done little for the Welsh and French morale to sit it out day after day staring at the superior English army. There were skirmishes, a few hundred soldiers died and then Owain retreated. Not since the Norman invasion had a French army sat in England, but the French, like the Welsh, would not do so again.

King Henry followed the retreating army but it was not an easy pursuit. Owain's scorched earth policy worked, and Henry's army was forced to disengage, starving. Henry regrouped at Hereford and invaded Wales for the fifth time, his intention being to stop the French from regaining their ships. He might have succeeded, but the Welsh winter turned on him again and the rivers filled, making the fords impassable. Some said that Owain conjured the storms for one final time against his old foe. Henry turned home in frustration and in October crossed from Wales to England yet again; but this was to be the last time.

In Wales the French managed to reach their ships and went home, although some French soldiers stayed behind to enjoy the cold rain and snow of a Welsh winter. They were homesick and miserable and they took it out on their host's lands and property. By the spring of 1406 when they too departed Wales was glad to be rid of them.

1406

The year opened badly for Owain. Providence delivered the heir to the throne of Scotland into Henry's hands when King Robert's son James was captured *en route* to France. With such a hostage Henry immediately secured his northern border.

It is to this time, early 1406, that the Tri-partite Indenture between Northumberland, Mortimer and Owain is assigned. Whether it was actually signed now, or had already been signed in 1405 is largely academic however, for the treaty was never much more than a scrap of paper. The three men promised each other every possible assistance – short of actual help.

What indeed had they to offer? Old Percy had fled to Scotland where the Scots, reluctantly accepting the necessity to be polite to Henry while he held their prince, offered to exchange him for the Earl of Douglas, held since Shrewsbury. Northumberland therefore fled the country, landing in Wales at Aberdaron in early 1406. He brought nothing but his name, though that might have been useful in fomenting rebellion in the north. All Mortimer had to offer was his nephew, the Earl of March, and he was in King Henry's hands. But Owain still had Wales.

The treaty was signed on 28 February, in either 1405 or 1406 – the latter date supported by the presence of all three men in Wales at that time. It is interesting as a historical document, particularly in the defining of the borders of the three new estates which would comprise England and Wales. It begins: 'In the first place that these lords, Owyn, the Earl and Edmund shall be mutually joined, confederated, united and bound by the band of true league and true friendship and sure and good union.' Which of them, one wonders, believed that in those treacherous times there was any more clamorous noise than a hollow ring to these words?

As if fearful of just such treachery, there is a long section on the need to be 'good and faithful friends' and the requirement of 'good faith'. To reinforce this second section a short third section is a résumé of it, labouring again the point that there should be mutual respect – 'Each of them, also, shall be content with that portion of the kingdom aforesaid, limited as below, without further exaction or superiority.'

The apportioning gave Northumberland the territory north of, and Mortimer the territory south of a line very roughly joining Kidderminster and Lowestoft. As far as Wales was concerned, however, Owain would have:

> the whole of Cambria or Wales, by the borders, limits and boundaries under-written, divided from Loegira, which is commonly called England; namely from the Severn Sea as the river Severn leads from the sea, going down to the north gate of the city of Worcester; and from that gate straight to the Ash tree, commonly called in the Cambrian or Welsh language Owen Margion, which grows on the highway from Bridgnorth to Kynvar [Kinver] thence by the highway direct, which is usually called the old or ancient way, to the head or source of the river Trent; hence to the head or source of the river Merse [Mersey]; hence as that river leads to the sea.

The treaty ends not with a restating of the need for friendship or good faith, but with a decision that should two of the parties fight, the third shall act as 'good and faithful counsel' whose decision on the quarrel would be final. It is clearly a document drawn up not by true friends but by fearful, suspicious allies brought together by a cause bigger than anything they could survive alone.

The use of the ash tree boundary marker was a necessity to Owain's bards, allowing them to spread the word that an ancient prophecy of Merlin was to be fulfilled. They cursed Henry, the 'mouldwarp cursed of God's own mouth'. A dragon, a wolf and a lion would come, their tails entwined. The Thames would be choked with corpses, England's rivers would run with blood and beneath the blood would drown the mouldwarp Henry.

Owain must have been aware that the treaty was largely worthless while his two co-signatories were in Wales with him, rather than in England preparing for the fight. Certainly, rather than rely on the help they could not hope to offer in the short term at least, Owain decided to renew overtures to the French. In early 1406 another parliament was held, probably again at Machynlleth, and from Pennal, a hamlet on the other side of the Dyfi, Owain wrote to Charles VI of France on 31 March.

In the letter Owain is quick to seize on the religious rift in Europe, the Papal Schism, which had caused a rival pope to be enthroned at Avignon. Owain promises that in his new Principality the Archbishop of St David's and all bishops will be appointed by France's Benedict XIII and not the Roman Gregory VII. At this point in the letter Owain includes a paragraph which makes a true statesman of the writer irrespective of the cant that precedes it and the hypocrisy that follows. He asks for permission to 'have two universities or places of general study, namely one in North Wales and the other in South Wales, in cities, towns or places to be hereafter decided and determined by our nuncios and ambassadors for that purpose'. Had Owain been successful in his struggle with the English, this far-sighted request would have given Wales its colleges before the Scots had theirs. It is to Owain's credit that even as he was struggling to maintain a free Wales, he could conceive of the need to plan for an educated generation of Welshmen.

After the call for universities, Owain comes to the point of his letter. Henry the usurper is accused of burning down churches and cathedrals and of slaughtering Welsh clergy and monks. King Charles is called on to sanction a crusade against Henry, for in addition to these sins against Holy Orders he is also a follower of the Roman pope. The Owain who wrote these comments on Henry was, of course, the man who had laid waste Abbey Cwmhir, St Asaph and a good number of other holy houses!

The letter to Francis is signed, 'Owensus Dei Gratia princeps

Walliae' and is dated in the 'sixth [year] of our reign'. Charles VI was delighted with Owain's letter and sent greetings and gifts – but he did not send an army.

As 1406 drew on, King Henry became ill, stricken with a disease which wasted his body and his mind. It may have been leprosy or syphilis, but whatever it was it left Prince Henry with a freer hand. He formed that free hand into a fist and prepared to punch Wales.

On St George's Day, Prince Henry was campaigning in Wales. Somewhere – history does not record exactly where – he met a force of Welshmen and killed a thousand of them. Another of Owain's sons died in this battle.

Prince Henry campaigned all over south Wales, for to leave Owain in the north would be to leave him free but isolated. Much of the country reverted to the king. The prince demanded heavy fines for their misdeeds, and the landowners paid readily. The alternative was probably bleak, but the irony was that south Wales' money now helped the English crown fight, while the north Wales country, ravaged continuously for so many years, could no longer sustain Owain's cause.

Owain still occupied the castles of Aberystwyth and Harlech, and on this Cardigan Bay coast he still held a regal court; one story tells of him exercising the royal prerogative of pardon over a felon. There are, in addition, many tales of Owain wandering the country, sometimes alone, sometimes with just a few followers. These stories are curious. Though as the days shortened to the end of 1406 and it was becoming clear that the Welsh were facing an uphill struggle just to survive, Owain still held sway over two-thirds of Wales. The tales are persistent: they tell of him living in a cave at the mouth of the Dysynni, not far south of Harlech, and in another cave on the side of Moel Hebog in Snowdonia. There is a story in an old manuscript that he was a guest of Sir Lawrence Berkrolles at his Coity castle. Sir Lawrence was an English knight and was reputedly struck dumb – literally, not just by the shock of the moment – when Owain shook his hand as he was leaving and revealed himself.

It would be easy to dismiss these stories, or to assume that they are misplaced in time from a period several years later when Owain really was on the run in Wales, but it is to this period that the following verses of Iolo Goch are said to relate:

> I saw with aching heart
> The golden dream depart;
> His glorious image in my mind,
> Was all that Owain left behind.
> Wild with despair and woebegone
> Thy faithful bard is left alone,
> To sigh, to weep, to groan.
>
> Thy sweet remembrance ever dear,
> Thy name still ushered by a tear,
> My inward anguish speak;
> How could'st thou, cruel Owain, go
> And leave the bitter tears to flow
> Down Gruffydd's furrowed cheek?

Gruffydd is a reference to Iolo's real name.

What was happening at this time? While it is true that Owain may well have had a price on his head, why should he have been wandering the countryside when his family had securely sheltered in Harlech castle? No satisfactory explanation can be given. Never again was Owain to be a threat, and indeed it is very difficult to actually catch sight of the Welsh prince from early 1406 onwards. Had the horror of the war and its failure taken away the reason of his cultured mind, leaving him a wandering, old, weary and confused man, or a man who for his own safety had to be escorted about in secret, so that his still-faithful followers could use his name to strike terror into their enemies?

Had he decided that he would return to his origins as the magical leader of the Welsh, and thus sought refuge in a cave to sleep out the years until he should come again?

Is it possible, even, that he was already dead . . . killed, murdered or worn out? No evidence for the remaining years of the rebellion ever satisfactorily explained his death or where he was buried.

1407 AND AFTER

The remaining rebellion was no glorious last stand on some bloodstained Gwynedd field. It died of starvation from lack of funds and men, and from the strangulation of the other Prince of Wales, Henry of Monmouth.

Prince Henry decided that Aberystwyth and Harlech, the castles that were still held by Owain, should be captured. With no firm base the Welsh could not hope to defend the country against the prince's combination of savagery and pardons – the stick and the carrot.

In the summer of 1407 Prince Henry besieged the old castle of Aberystwyth, beautifully set beside the sea. By an irony of fate, beside the ruins of the castle there now stands a college of the University of Wales. But in 1407 what stood there were two cannons, the newest weapon in the royal armoury. The castle garrison, used to the old-fashioned siege engines some of which were also present, must have looked at these new machines with curiosity, though doubtless their wonder did not survive the first bombardment.

Seven cannons were brought in all, including the king's 'gonne', a four-and-a-half-ton monster, and the 'Messenger'. With them came five hundredweight of powder, nearly nine hundredweight of saltpetre and three hundredweight of sulphur. The cannon pounded the walls of the castle, terrifying the garrison. But the cannoniers were also terrified, one of the 'gonnes' bursting during the siege and killing everyone close to it.

The siege continued until mid-September when Owain's castle commander, Rhys Ddu, offered Prince Henry a curious compromise whereby there would be a truce until 24 October, when fighting would recommence. If by 1 November the castle had not been relieved, then the garrison would surrender. A treaty to that effect was agreed and Prince Henry removed his men to Strata Florida before returning to England. There he received the grateful thanks of Parliament. As he did so, Owain reinforced the castle and cancelled the treaty.

The winter of 1407–8 was one of the worst for many years: raw, pitiless wind and bitter cold, with the whole land under a carpet of snow from Christmas until March. To add to the Welsh misery, late in 1407 the Duke of Orleans, their champion at the French king's court, was murdered in France. In the wake of the killing, England and France signed a truce. Now the English crown was free of threats from Scotland and France. Then in early 1408 the old Earl of Northumberland attempted one last uprising and was killed at the battle of Branham Moor. What few hopes the Welsh may have had as 1407 came to an end, died in the freezing start to 1408.

There were some minor revolts when the summer sun had removed the snows from the land of Wales and strangely these were in Glamorgan, the first area to have accepted the royal pardon. The heavy fines imposed by the crown caused ill-feeling and this was played upon by the northern rebels. But it was too late for the men of Glamorgan to find that the devil they did not know was no better than the one they knew. The rebels were ousted and the heavy hand of England strengthened its grip. In the north the castles of Aberystwyth and Harlech were again under siege and with no relief possible from land or sea the constant bombardment of Prince Henry's forces eventually broke the spirit of the defenders. Late in 1408 Aberystwyth fell, and then in 1409 Harlech, the last redoubt, surrendered.

Within Harlech's walls, Edmund Mortimer had died, and at its surrender Owain's wife and the last of his children were taken. Chivalry prevailed however and Owain's family were taken unharmed to London. Later, it is believed, Margaret Glyndwr returned to Wales to live out her life with one of her daughters. For the rest, the Welsh were treated leniently – Prince Henry had astutely noted that the pardon worked better than the sword. There were other brief skirmishes in later years but never the decisive final defeat that signalled an end to the rebellion. Perhaps the true end came after a raid on the Shropshire border in 1410, when from the Red Castle at Welshpool a band of English emerged to crush the raiding party. Rhys Ddu and Rhys ap Tudor were taken prisoner – as was Philip Scudamore, an Owain sympathizer from Herefordshire. After the custom of the day, following the inevitable executions the head of Scudamore was spiked at Shrewsbury, that of Rhys the Black at Chester and that of Rhys ap Tudor at London.

Along the border and in England's capital, the blackening heads of his last generals told of Owain's defeat.

Of Owain himself nothing certain is known from about 1406 and nothing at all from 1412. Prince Henry of Monmouth succeeded his father and became Henry V on 21 March 1413. In July 1415 the new king offered a pardon to Owain and any of his men who remained free. There was no reply. In February 1416 the king tried again, using Owain's son Maredudd as an intermediary. This certainly implies that Owain was still alive, though Maredudd may not have known this for certain when he accepted his assignment. This new offer was not taken up either, though Maredudd himself did accept a pardon in 1417. By then Owain would have been at least fifty-eight years old – no great age by our standards but we do not expose ourselves to the chronic Welsh weather and the worries of war. Perhaps Owain was dead.

Certainly Iolo Goch thought so:

> and when thy evening sun is set,
> may grateful Cambria ne'er forget,
> Its morning rays, but on thy tomb,
> May never-fading laurels bloom.

Kentchurch

There were some who believed that Owain went to live with his daughter Alice and her husband John Scudamore in Herefordshire's Golden Valley. There are several versions of this story. One has Owain taking the living of Kentchurch church and dying there; the priest Sion (John) of Kentchurch was a poet and had a reputation as a mystic. There is a fifteenth-century painting of the priest in Kentchurch Court, showing an old, weary man with sunken, staring eyes. Another version has Owain dying at Monnington Court, a mile or two northward. It would be a sad irony if either of these places held his body, for each is in England and but a short distance from Grosmont Castle, whence Prince Henry of Monmouth had emerged one day in 1405 to sign the death warrant of the rebellion with a crushing victory.

Confusion was added to the story of Owain's death when it was announced that his grave had been found at Monnington. But not Monnington Court – Monnington-on-Wye, northward yet again. The confusion arose because of the similarity of name and this is often quoted. One author from early this century not only maintained that the Wye village was Owain's resting place, but gave the date of his death as 20 September 1415!

There were others who maintained he did not die in the peace of his daughters' house but lonely, cold and weary on an exposed ridge in Gwynedd, or in the woods of Glamorgan.

The bards depicted him sleeping with his men in some concealed cave, awaiting the time when they should rise again to rid the country of the English. True the story is Arthurian but such was the Celtic need for some hope, so utter was their desolation.

WALES UNTIL 1536

In the aftermath of the rebellion of Owain Glyndwr, the English Parliament enacted laws which were framed to ensure that never again could the Welsh threaten an English king. If savage laws had not been sufficient to hold them down when rebellion threatened, then clearly what were needed were laws that were even more savage and repressive. No man of Welsh parentage could buy land near a Marcher town, or be a citizen of such a town, or hold any office at all, or possess a weapon. No Welsh child could be apprenticed to trade or go to college. If there were lawsuits between an Englishman and a Welshman, then Englishmen must be judge and jury. If any Englishman were foolish enough to marry a Welshwoman, he would become Welsh in the eyes of the law. And finally, all gatherings of Welsh people were forbidden.

This last law was the most brutal because it denied the Welsh the opportunity to help each other at harvest. Their country had been ravaged, their sons killed. They were to be taxed to pay for the cost of the war – and now they could harvest no food. As if all that was not enough, Wales was home to many who had been raiders all their adult life and could not – or would not – stop.

Yet when Henry V who had smashed the rebellion called for men to fight for him in France, the old desire for a warrior king to love and admire was still strong, and Welsh bowmen won for him the battle of Agincourt. Henry V was a brilliant general: fearless and, best of all, victorious – a man every Celt could be proud to follow.

Not so Henry's son, Henry VI, who succeeded him when only nine months old. The long-term government of the state by a council of ministers left England full of ambitious lords, none more so than Richard Plantaganet, Duke of York, son of the sister of the Earl of March, whose uncle Edmund Mortimer had died for Glyndwr in Harlech Castle. In the power struggle that followed – the Wars of the Roses as it has become known – Wales saw action as an army raised by Owen and Jasper Tudor, and marched across country from Pembroke to face defeat at Mortimer's Cross.

West Wales was staunchly Lancastrian and was invaded by land and sea for its beliefs; Jasper Tudor, having survived the battle, fled to Ireland. It is an irony that a descendant of the Mortimer family which sided with Glyndwr should have been in a position to chastise a part of the country that so vigorously opposed his rebellion.

The Wars of the Roses had begun with the vacuum left by Henry V, that most powerful of kings, defeater of Glyndwr and conqueror of France. After he died, his young widow, Catherine of France, married a commoner – Owen Tudor of the Anglesey family who had captured Conwy castle and supported Glyndwr. They had two children, Edmund and Jasper, the Earls of Richmond and Pembroke, legitimized by an Act of Parliament in 1453. Edmund Tudor married Margaret Beaufort, a descendant of John of Gaunt and heiress to the title of the family who had given England Henry IV. Their son Henry Tudor was raised in France, since his existence represented a threat to Edward IV, the Yorkist king. When Edward died in 1483, his brother Richard III took the throne, entering history as the evil hunchback who murdered his nephews and rightful heirs to the throne, the 'Princes in the Tower'.

On 7 August 1485 Henry Tudor landed in Pembrokeshire, and the Welsh rose to herald a new Welsh star rising to rescue them from oppression. The bards could recite the lineage of this Welshman and point out the prophecies which foretold his coming and the victory that was bound to be his. Henry Tudor travelled north through Cardiganshire to Machynlleth, the Parliament town of Owain Glyndwr. He then moved east through Powys to Welshpool and on to Shrewsbury and England. On 22 August he met Richard III at Bosworth. With Richard's defeat the Welsh gave England a king, Henry VII.

Fifty years later the second king of the house of Tudor, Henry VIII, united England and Wales. In the Act of Union Welshmen were given equal rights to Englishmen, since all became citizens of the new kingdom. English law was brought to Wales, replacing the laws of Hywel Dda, but replacing also the summary justice of the Marcher lords. In only one respect was the Union obviously against the interests of the Welsh – the English language was made the official and only language of the courts and administrators. In the nineteenth century 'the Welsh' existed in some schools – given to a child who spoke Welsh, who in turn passed it on to the next child to do so. At the end of the week whichever child had the stick ('the Welsh') was beaten with it. As a result children sneaked about at night to hear Welsh being spoken behind closed doors and curtains. But like the Welsh themselves, their language refused to be broken on the English wheel, fighting a dogged rearguard action in the mountains of Gwynedd, to appear victorious four and half centuries later when its presence was acknowledged and it was given joint status.

WHAT PRICE REBELLION?

When Owain Glyndwr emerged from relative obscurity in 1399 he was a prosperous, cultured country gentleman, living in a Wales which, though moved by undercurrents of resentment against its English overlords, was not striving for rebellion. When he drifted back into obscurity a dozen years later, he was a penniless rebel leaving a country ravaged by hard years of brutal warfare.

In those cold terms Owain's achievements were negative, both for himself and for the nation he led. What was it that he was seeking to achieve, and why did he fail?

He had taken charge of a country of which only half – the lands of Gwynedd and Powys – had wholeheartedly supported him, and which was a maze of intrigue and strange interests built up over a century of alien domination. To advance his cause he had at his disposal a mass of untrained farm-boys, while his officers were in the main given to 'rushes of blood'. Gerald of Wales – a Norman priest to be sure, but one who knew the Welsh – had summed up their fighting qualities in a sentence: 'In the first attack the Welsh are more than men, in the second less than women.'

Recognizing their lack of training and the deficiencies in their fighting qualities, Owain had fought the only campaign that offered any hope of success. He dared not fight the English army in open battle, for that army was trained in the fields of France where they had humbled a nation whose resources far outstripped those of Wales. What chance did his outnumbered and lightly-clad warriors stand in the field? Better to have them roaming the country, picking off stragglers from the invading army as it lumbered about, huge and slow.

To have an invading army in Wales at all was to risk being cornered by accident or by bribe, and so the country must be altered so that it could not be held or occupied by the invader. To which end Owain stripped the country bare, removing the wealth that might equip an invading force, the food that might feed it and anything that might shelter it. This scorched earth policy which – virtually of necessity – included the looting of all major towns and of the monastic houses, has always been a matter of contention amongst those who speak of the rebellion. There is evidence that in the early years, however, when the profits of looting were large, Owain gave money to those who had suffered hardship from his policies, and there is evidence too that not all the raids were meant to be as vicious as they turned out to be. It is also true that we live in times so far removed from medieval Wales that it is difficult to understand whether Owain's chosen policy was so strange for the period in which he lived. The English had invented scorched earth in France to prevent their army being followed across country by the French troops. To move an army of many thousands at that time meant having to live off the land, for transport was too slow to provide a continuous stream of supplies from a rear storage dump. Perhaps the Welsh who had been with the English kings in France had learned how best to prevent themselves from being pursued.

Of course scorched earth as a defence policy does not imply automatically that the devastation did not matter to those whose land was scorched. It is true that medieval Wales was not, as it is today, a land where reasonably prosperous citizens had nice homes full of expensive luxuries. But even if the loss of their pitiable few possessions could be made good in a short time, and even if they could survive until next year's harvest, the suffering among the native Welsh was appalling. Neither does the requirement of scorched earth justify some of the more extreme killings, of Welshmen believed to be pro-English, or the desecration of bodies as at Pilleth, or Owain's refusal to allow safe passage to the womenfolk of Carreg Cennen castle when his army reached it. Even in medieval times, you did not make war on women.

Perhaps again Owain was seeking to ensure not only that the English understood that Wales was no place for them, but also that it was no place for anyone likely to offer them support or shelter. Ironically it was the scorched earth and the associated savagery which eventually lost his cause; the people and the very land of Wales became war-weary, tired of endless carnage, despair and poverty . . . tired eventually of Glyndwr. What they wanted was peace and it became obvious that only the English crown could offer them that. When you are starving, what you want is food. When you are wounded by an English spear in your belly, what you want is to live. Ideals are for the well-fed and for the survivors.

It would have been different had Owain been able to fight just one decisive battle which would have assured his compatriots that he was capable not only of keeping the English out but of keeping them out for good. With his own troops he could not achieve that, and his attempts to do so with a French army were bound to fail. The Welsh did not like the French any more than they liked the English; it was merely that at the time they disliked them less. The remnant French army which over-wintered in Wales soon proved Welsh suspicions of foreigners to be justified. The alliance was based on falsehoods. Wales wanted France to conquer England and then to go away, and France only needed Wales to offer it a land route to England. Ultimately, if the invasion had been successful, Owain would have found, like Vortigern before him, that the problem with invited armies is that they stay.

The same comments can also be made about the Tri-partite Indenture. This virtually had written into its text the intrigue and discord that would have been the inevitable result of the success of the alliance of signatories at the battle of Shrewsbury.

But these are all negative qualities. It is important to stress the positive element of the Pennal Manifesto and, therefore, of Owain's ambitions for his free principality. His desire for Welsh universities is of the greatest importance and shows that Owain recognized two things. The first was that, to be free of England in the fullest sense, Wales had to provide and maintain its own government, which in turn required the education of a whole generation of Welshmen. Owain had been concerned that the Welsh at Oxford should think well of him and had, in fact, given money to many of those who joined him. Secondly, he recognized that education was the way to free men's minds and that what the Welsh needed was a change of attitude, a new way of thinking. Too long they had been the slaves of the English. Owain would educate the young Welsh and send them home to teach not only their own children, but also their parents. Owain's universities were a profound desire.

It was said in Tudor times that once when Owain was out walking from Glyndyfrdwy very early in the morning, he met the Abbot of Valle Crucis Abbey, also taking the early morning air. When Owain joked that the abbot had risen early, the abbot said no – it was Owain who had risen early . . . a century too early.

It is a lovely story, but it takes no account of the real Owain Glyndwr. It implies that, though he may have been the right man, he came at the wrong time. In retrospect we can see that failure to achieve a goal does not render the goal unworthy. Owain Glyndwr's gift to the Welsh was the idea that the people are greater than the prince.

Selected Reading

OWAIN GLYNDWR

ALLDAY, HELEN D., *Insurrection in Wales*, T. Dalton, Suffolk, 1981

BRADLEY, ARTHUR GRANVILLE, *Owen Glyndwr, and the Last Struggle for Welsh Independence, with a Brief Sketch of Welsh History*, G. P. Putnam, London, 1901

DAVIES, JOHN DAVID GRIFFITH, *Owen Glyn Dwr*, Eric Partridge, London, 1934

JONES, GWILYM ARTHUR, *Owen Glyndwr*, University of Wales Press, Cardiff, 1962

PHILLIPS, DAVID RHYS, *A Selected Bibliography of Owen Glyndwr*, published by the author in Swansea, 1915

SKIDMORE, IAN, *Owain Glyndwr: Prince of Wales*, Christopher Davies, Swansea, 1978

WILLIAMS, GLANMOR, *Owen Glendower*, Clarendon Biographies, Oxford University Press, 1966

WELSH HISTORY AND FOLKLORE

JACK, IAN R., *Medieval Wales*, The Sources of History with Hodder and Stoughton, 1972

OWEN, REV. ELIAS, *Welsh Folk Lore*, Woodall, Minshall & Co., 1887

OWEN, TREFOR M., *Welsh Folk Customs*, National Museum of Wales, 1959

REES, WILLIAM, *An Historial Atlas of Wales from Early to Modern Times*, Faber & Faber, 1951

RHYS, JOHN, *Celtic Folklore: Welsh and Manx*, Clarendon Press, Oxford, 1901

RODERICK, A. J., (ED.), *Wales through the Ages*, in two volumes, Christopher Davies, 1959

THE COUNTRYSIDE AND ARCHITECTURE

BRADLEY, A. G., *Highways and Byways in North Wales*, Macmillan, 1898

CONDRY, WILLIAM, *The Natural History of Wales*, Collins New Naturalist, 1981

HILLING, JOHN B., *The Historic Architecture of Wales*, University of Wales Press, 1976

PHILLIPS, PAULINE, *A View of Old Montgomeryshire*, Christopher Davies, 1977

TILLOTSON, JOHN, *Picturesque Scenery in Wales*, T. J. Allman, 1861, reproduced in fascimile by Stewart Williams, 1972

LITERARY REFERENCE

GANTZ, JEFFERY (translator), *The Mabinogion*, Penguin, 1976

JACKSON, KENNETH HURLSTONE (translator), *A Celtic Miscellany*, Penguin, 1971. This includes the elegy to Llywelyn ap Gruffydd by Gruffydd ab yr Ynad Coch

SHAKESPEARE, WILLIAM, *Henry IV*, Part One, Penguin, 1968

JOURNALS

These journals, all held at the National Library of Wales, Aberystwyth, contain articles of interest about Owain Glyndwr and places in Powys:

Archaeologia Cambrensis
Bulletin of the Board of Celtic Studies
Transactions of the Radnorshire Society
Montgomeryshire Collections
Powys Land Club
Theses of the University of Wales

Index